T0208897

The
VOICE *in the* CUP

What's in Your Cup?

Dr. Benedita Monteiro Gomes

WESTBOW
PRESS®
A DIVISION OF THOMAS NELSON
& ZONDERVAN

WestBow Press books may be ordered through booksellers or by contacting:

WestBow Press
A Division of Thomas Nelson & Zondervan
1663 Liberty Drive
Bloomington, IN 47403
www.westbowpress.com
1 (866) 928-1240

Scripture taken from the King James Version of the Bible.

Scripture taken from the New King James Version®. Copyright © 1982 by Thomas Nelson. Used by permission. All rights reserved.

ISBN: 978-1-9736-8455-8 (sc)
ISBN: 978-1-9736-8454-1 (hc)
ISBN: 978-1-9736-8456-5 (e)

Library of Congress Control Number: 2020901560

Print information available on the last page.

WestBow Press rev. date: 02/06/2020

CONTENTS

DEDICATION

This book is dedicated with much love and admiration to my beautiful and amazing mother Zuilda Fermino Monteiro Gomes and to my wonderful father João Nepomuceno Gomes who sacrificed their lives and immigrated to the United States of America, so I could have the "American dream". Obrigadinha Mamá ma Djão!

ACKNOWLEDGEMENT

I wish to acknowledge my deepest gratitude and appreciation to my daughter and friend Bobbie Monteiro Jean for her support in editing this book, and to Dr. Haga, Advisor for all her wisdom and encouragement during my studies at New Life Bible College and Seminary. I also wish the acknowledge Pastor Faith Carroll, Elder Michael Spruill and my niece Ondina Duarte for their support in the integrity of this book. In addition, I acknowledge my friend Dr. Doretha Cale for painting the perfect book cover.

A PRAYER FOR THE READER

Dear heavenly Father, I come to you in Jesus's name covered in His precious blood, knowing that as you look at the mercy seat, the blood of your Son Jesus Christ cries out on my behalf. Father, I know you hear my every prayer, always. Thank you for hearing my prayers. Father, I know this because I join the intercessors—Jesus Christ your Son and your precious Holy Spirit—in intercession, and together we pray your will for your beloved people. It is with a pure heart and clean hands that I present this book inspired by you and pray that you open your people's spiritual eyes as they read this book so they can see the blessings that your Son Jesus Christ has provided for all who believe in Him and accept His teachings. I pray the blood of Jesus will cleanse them from all unrighteousness and make them whole in the Beloved. Thank you, Father, that all godly prayers begin with you and they are yes and amen! *"For God so loved the world that he gave his only begotten Son, that whosoever believeth in him should not perish, but have everlasting life"* (John 3:16 KJV).

INTRODUCTION

We live in a time when most people do not want to talk, teach, or preach about the blood of Jesus. Once in a blue moon, there may be a blood song or two sung or played in a service. Communion is not offered as often as it used to be, and many lack in knowledge and preparation for the partaking of this awesome act of obedience. Regardless of what one chooses to think, the blood exists and has not lost its power, nor will it ever lose it. The blood of Jesus is the difference between religion and relationship. Without the blood of Jesus Christ, there is no remission of sins. We find all we need in the blood of Christ; thus, Satan does not want people to know about or believe in it. The blood is the power of God to redeem His people.

Often, people believe the lie that if they do not believe in something, it does not exist. No, it exists; you just will not benefit from it to the fullest. The shed blood of Christ is no different. Those who believe are saved, healed, and delivered, and they walk in freedom and liberty. They are no longer slaves to Satan; rather, they are sons and daughters of the most-high God with permanent residency in heaven. They are citizens of heaven.

It is my prayer that you read this book with an open mind to the truth of the living God and allow yourself to experience the benefits of the shed blood of His Son Christ Jesus, the cup of salvation. In it there is salvation, healing, deliverance, and provision for whatever you need now and will ever need. There is a voice in each cup, and I pray you forsake all other cups and choose this day to drink from His holy communion cup. Cheers!

– 1 –

Attributes of Human Blood

To understand this study, you must begin by asking the following questions: What is blood? What is a cup? And what are the substances in each cup?

Blood is indispensable to life, and the Bible clearly states that life is in the blood: "For the life of the flesh *is* in the blood: and I have given it to you upon the altar to make an atonement for your souls: for it *is* the blood *that* maketh an atonement for the soul" (Lev. 17:11 KJV). Blood circulates through our bodies and delivers vital substances such as oxygen and nutrients to our bodies' cells. In addition, it transports metabolic waste products away from those cells. There is no substitute for blood. It cannot be duplicated or manufactured. Hence the need for blood donors, for we are the only source of human blood.

There are four basic attributes of human blood—red blood cells, white blood cells, plasma, and platelets. Red blood cells make up 40 to 45 percent of our blood volume. They are generated from the bone marrow at a rate of four to five billion per hour and have a life cycle of approximately 120 days in the body. Although white blood cells account for only about 1 percent of our blood, they are very important. White blood cells are essential for good health and protection against sickness and disease. Like red blood cells, they are constantly being generated from our bone marrow. They flow through the bloodstream and attack foreign bodies, comparable to viruses and bacteria. They can even leave the bloodstream to extend the fight into tissue.

Plasma is the liquid portion of blood. It is yellowish in color and is made up mostly of water, but it also contains proteins, sugars, hormones, and salts. It carries water and nutrients to our body's tissues. Platelets are an amazing part of blood. They are the smallest of our blood cells and literally look like plates in their inactive form. Platelets control bleeding. Wherever a wound occurs, the blood vessel will send out a signal. Platelets receive that signal, travel to the area, and transform into their active formation, growing long tentacles to contact with the vessel and form clusters to plug the wound until it heals. (https://www.oneblood.org/about-donating/target-your-type/)

It's no wonder there are eight different blood types, and each one holds an exceptional power to save lives and to give people a second chance. The number 8 represents a new beginning or a new life. I remember when my mother was very sick, weak, and dying; however, after a blood transfusion, she regained her strength and lived many more years—thanks to the gift of blood, or life. This is an example of how important human blood is to individuals.

Knowing this facilitates your learning of the blood of Jesus Christ and its importance in your abundant life, for it has paid for your eternal life. Death can be purchased only with blood, nothing else. The blood of Jesus is the power of the cross and of God because it is the ultimate sacrifice—the only sacrifice that met the qualifications of the perfect and holy sacrifice.

According to a study by M. R. DeHaan, MD, the blood in the body of a fetus is separate from that of the mother, and it never mixes. The blood comes from the father, and the egg from the mother provides the beginning of the flesh of the baby. This is the reason Jesus's blood was pure and holy: it came from the Holy Spirit, His heavenly Father. Even though His flesh, or physical body, may seem to have come from His earthly mother, Virgin Mary, it was prepared by God. Therefore, it could not see or experience corruption. "He seeing this before spake of the resurrection of Christ, that his soul was not left in hell, neither his flesh did see corruption" (Acts 2:31 KJV). This is how Jesus was man and God at the same time—pure and holy, without any sin whatsoever. Jesus's flesh was different from ours because it was prepared for Him by God Himself. It was without sin and without blemish and without corruption.

> Wherefore when he cometh into the world, he saith, Sacrifice and offering thou wouldest not, but a body hast thou prepared me. (Heb. 10:5 KJV)

> For unto us a child is born, unto us a son is given: and the government shall be upon his shoulder: and his name shall be called Wonderful, Counsellor, the mighty God, the everlasting Father, the Prince of Peace. (Isa. 9:6 KJV)

Jesus the child grew up to become Jesus the man, but He was Jesus the Son of God. He is God Himself before conception, at conception, at birth, and after birth. It was His holy blood and only His blood that could redeem humankind to God because Jesus's blood is incorruptible.

> Knowing that you were not redeemed with corruptible things, *like* silver or gold, from your aimless conduct *received* by tradition from your fathers, but with the precious blood of Christ, as of a lamb without blemish and without spot. (1 Peter 1:18–19 NKJV; italics added)

No other blood will do. However, you have the choice to accept or reject Jesus's life sacrifice. So my questions to you at this point are, What cup is speaking to you—the cup of the Lord or the cup of demons—and from what cup will you drink?

Let's examine the different types of cups before making the decision to pick up, lift up, and indulge in drinking from the wrong one. The Bible says, "My people are destroyed for lack of knowledge: because thou hast rejected knowledge, I will also reject thee, that thou shalt be no priest to me: seeing thou hast forgotten the law of thy God, I will also forget thy children" (Hosea 4:6 KJV). Let this not be said of you, but rather, embrace the wisdom that the Word of God imparts to you and welcome the knowledge so you may not be rejected by your God and King.

– 2 –

Vessels of Honor and of Dishonor

Throughout the Bible the cup functions as a symbol for an individual, a people, or a nation's fate. What's in the cup can be positive or negative, as seen in scriptures, based on blessings or curses according to attitudes and behaviors toward God, His Word, and His commands. You find innumerable blessings from trusting and obeying the Word of God, and you will also find curses from disobedience to Him and to His Word. Obedience is better than sacrifice.

> Now go and smite Amalek, and utterly destroy
> all that they have, and spare them not; but slay
> both man and woman, infant and suckling, ox
> and sheep, camel and ass. (1 Sam. 15:3 KJV)

> And Samuel said, Hath the LORD as great
> delight in burnt offerings and sacrifices, as in
> obeying the voice of the LORD? Behold, to
> obey is better than sacrifice, and to hearken
> than the fat of rams. (1 Sam. 15:22 KVJ)

Do not be like King Saul, who was rejected as king because he failed to destroy the Amalekites by choosing to keep the best spoils for himself and even sacrificing some to God. All God required of King Saul was obedience. He did not want animal sacrifice. This act of disobedience cost King Saul the kingdom and not only for him but also his family line. As I study scriptures throughout the Bible, I see how God is pleased with and blesses those who obey Him and how disobedience opens doors for Satan to torment God's people. This is another reason it is so important to stay under the umbrella of God's love continuously. All the enemy needs is a crack in the wall to enter in and cause havoc in your life. Some say it is impossible to please God, but I say hold on to God's unchanging hands, and you will be more than conquerors.

> Know in all these things we are more than
> conquerors through him who loved us. For
> I am convinced that neither death nor life,
> neither angels nor demons, neither the present
> nor the future, nor any powers, neither height
> nor depth, nor anything else in all creation,
> will be able to separate us from the love of God
> that is in Christ Jesus our Lord. He will not
> let you fall, nor stumble. (Rom. 7:37–39 KJV)

You have nothing to fear, but you do have God to regard with reverence. He is not asking you to do the impossible. That is His job. All He is asking of you is to listen to His voice and to trust and obey Him. It is that simple. Humans love to make things more complicated than they are. They are just looking for an excuse to disobey. Disobey God and your cup will be a vessel of dishonor. Obey God and your cup will be a vessel of honor.

According to the apostle Paul, there are different vessels—some of honor and some of dishonor. "But in a great house there are not only vessels of gold and of silver, but also of wood and of earth; and some to honour, and some to dishonour" (2 Tim. 2:20 KJV). When you look at the materials mentioned, you see that gold and silver are most costly and are referred to as "vessels of honor" and used for special occasions. Wood and clay are less expensive and referred to as "vessels of dishonor" and are used daily. Therefore, if you want to become a vessel of honorable use, you must clean up all self-impurities in preparation for God's greater use. Many times, we cry out to God to use us for His glory while we live in chaos. When we look at our lives, we find inside our cups many undesirable, even detestable, things that hinder our relationship with our Lord and Savior. Our bodies are the temple of the Holy Spirit, and they must be free of debris from the storms of life." Know ye not that ye are the temple of God, and that the Spirit of God dwelleth in you? If any man defiles the temple of God, him shall God destroy; for the temple of God is holy, which temple ye are" (1 Cor. 3:16–17 KJV). It must be holy for He is holy.

You may have been through unspeakable things, of no fault of your own. We live in a fallen world. Bad things happen to good people, you may have heard many in your circles say. But, truth be told, we are all bad and have done some bad things, for the Bible states that all have sinned.

> Therefore, we are all in need of the Savior, Jesus Christ. "For all have sinned and come short of the glory of God." (Rom. 3:23 KJV)

It behooves us not to pass judgment, rather to help one another. There is a proverb in my native tongue that reads and translates as follows: *Uma mão lava a outra e ambos vão au rosto*, or "One hand washes the other and both wash the face." That is, instead of spending time pointing fingers, we should be helping one another get straight with God. Many invest too much time working with and for the enemy under the control of a viper spirit that they forget and neglect their identity in Christ.

> And when they were escaped, then they knew that the island was called Melita. And the barbarous people shewed us no little kindness: for they kindled a fire, and received us everyone, because of the present rain, and because of the cold. And when Paul had gathered a bundle of sticks, and laid *them* on the fire, there came a viper out of the heat, and fastened on his hand. And when the barbarians saw the *venomous* beast hang on his hand, they said among

themselves, No doubt this man is a murderer, whom, though he hath escaped the sea, yet vengeance suffereth not to live. And he shook off the beast into the fire and felt no harm. Howbeit they looked when he should have swollen, or fallen down dead suddenly: but after they had looked a great while, and saw no harm come to him, they changed their minds, and said that he was a god. (Acts 28:1–6 KJV)

These are people who inject spiritual venom into their victims, and many young in the Lord and the naive have fallen prey to this spirit. Jesus called such people a brood of vipers. "You brood of vipers! how can you speak good, when you are evil? For out of the abundance of the heart the mouth speaks" (Matt. 12:34; see Matt. 12:24–28, 31–34 KJV).

The heart is the center of life and of your cup; therefore, you must clean it and keep it holy. You cannot speak good things if your heart is filled with poisonous venom because out of the abundance of the heart the mouth speaks. You know that bitter and sweet water cannot come from the same fountain or cup. Many are sick and dying because they have not learned the art of heart cleaning and maintenance of a clear, clean, and pure heart and conscience. Then, they are not able to discern between conviction and condemnation. If fact, I have heard these two words used as if they are the same. "Doth a fountain send forth at the same place sweet water and bitter?" (James 3:11 KJV)

Conviction comes from the Holy Spirit, and it is meant to help you acknowledge your wrongdoing, repent, ask for forgiveness, receive forgiveness from the Lord, forgive yourself for the wrong you have done, and turn away from that which caused you the breakdown in relationship with people and with your Lord and God. Conviction is intended for restoration and not guilt and condemnation.

Condemnation, on the other hand, comes from Satan. It is intended to make you feel guilty and hopeless. Its intent is to destroy, kill, and rob you and to cause you to hate God, your only source of deliverance. It is never good, and it has destructive powers. It is crucial that you know and understand the difference between the two, and should you feel condemned, you must reach out to a trusted individual for help. Do not entertain the lie, or you are sure to find yourself in the snare set before you by the enemy and be punished, for that is his doing, and he is excellent at evil. That's his job. Remember, he came to do damage, but Jesus came to give you life more abundantly. "The thief cometh not, but for to steal, and to kill, and to destroy: I am come that they might have life, and that they might have it more abundantly" (John 10:10 KJV). You must live a life full of vibrancy and vitality because Jesus is "the author and finisher of your faith. "Looking unto Jesus, the author and finisher of *our* faith, who for the joy that was set before Him endured the cross, despising the shame, and has sat down at the right hand of the throne of God" (Heb. 12:2 KJV). You do not have to listen to or fear the lies of the enemy. Jesus is on your side. He paid for your sins on the cross, and He is your intercessor still today.

"Who is he that condemneth? It is Christ that died, yea rather, that is risen again, who is even at the right hand of God, who also maketh intercession for us." (Rom. 8:34 KJV). Listen, He died for you. Why would He condemn you? No! He loves you, and He prays for you continuously. He prays you keep your cup clean and make it to paradise with Him someday soon. He said that He went before you to prepare a place for you, and He will come back to receive you. "And if I go and prepare a place for you, I will come again, and receive you unto myself; that where I am, there ye may be also" (John 14:3 KJV). He did not leave you comfortless. He sent His precious Holy Spirit to teach and to guide you, to lead you into all truth, and to comfort you in all situations. Jesus is coming back soon. "If ye love me, keep my commandments. And I will pray the Father, and he shall give you another Comforter, that he may abide with you for ever; Even the Spirit of truth; whom the world cannot receive, because it seeth him not, neither knoweth him: but ye know him; for he dwelleth with you and shall be in you. I will not leave you comfortless: I will come to you" (John 14:15–18 KJV). You must keep His Word in your heart. If your heart is filled with the Word of God, there will not be room for anything else. Then, Jesus will truly be the Lord of your life, the center of your attention, and Satan will have nothing in you, as he did not have anything in Jesus. Only then will your cup be suitable for God's honorable use. Those who trust and obey God will be taught by His Holy Spirit, the teacher. Trust Him and trust in Him.

The Lord taught me this lesson through a disease. I never was angry at the person who infected me with the disease. The entire time, I just prayed for the person and put him in the Lord's hands. After all, he was a slave to Satan and his dirty work. If you pause to think that, at one time or another, all have been enslaved by Satan and deputized to do his dirty work, you would be quick to forgive as Jesus taught us to do. "And forgive us our debts, as we forgive our debtors" (Matt. 6:12 KJV). You must give the same mercy you expect God to give to you. That is the way forgiveness works. You cannot expect God to forgive you if you are not willing to forgive others. The Word of God is clear. It is in the process of forgiving others that your sins are forgiven and you are healed. It is not science. It is just obedience to God's Word. I know sometimes it is difficult to forgive those who have hurt you. However, by not forgiving them, you stay in bondage and, believe it or not, they are still in control of your life. Is it worth staying in bondage? I think not. Just let go, and let the Lord heal your heart and your life.

Forgiveness is the key to a clean and pure heart. Daily, people say and do things that can offend and hurt you intentionally and unintentionally, and if you allow those things to reach your heart, you can be wounded and offended. The spirit of offense is slowly killing God's people. Do not let your guard down, because the enemy uses those closest to you; they are the ones who can hurt you the most and can do instant damage. You need to be sharp and on guard not against people, but against the tactics of the enemy. You must not fall prey to the enemy's trap. You must be vigilant and in continuous prayer with a clean and pure heart. When you have a pure heart and clean hands, God can perform His miracles so clearly shown in His Word in your life. He can heal you and He can deliver you because, like Jesus, the enemy has nothing in you. "Hereafter I will not talk much with you: for the prince of this world cometh, and hath nothing in me" (John 14:30 KJV). Jesus is our example, and when you do like He did and you live like He lived, then you can say as He said: "The prince of this world has nothing in me." Following Jesus's instruction, I was healed from an incurable disease, and I have documentation to prove it to the skeptical. This lesson for me was one that I will treasure forever. I have put it to use in my teachings, and it works for all who are not ashamed to follow this teaching.

I have ministered and continue to minister nationally and internationally. One day as I ministered in prayer after the preaching of the Word of the Lord, I had a group of wounded women come to me for prayer. The Lord instructed me to tell them to kneel at the altar and to stay there until they had forgiven everybody who had ever hurt them. They were not to get up for prayer until they had taken care of business, and each one of them obeyed the Word of the Lord. After they got up and I prayed for them, they were all healed. Even blind eyes were opened. Praise the Lord! I find that forgiveness is a beautiful thing. Don't you?

How good does it feel when you have been forgiven? It is the same way the person who offended you feels. Better yet, once you have forgiven those people, they no longer hold you hostage. As you hold onto the act, the act holds on tightly to you. Forgive and let go, and you will see, feel, and experience a freedom that you have never known before. That is why it is so vitally important to keep short accounts or, better yet, empty accounts when it comes to the sin of unforgiveness. Oh, yes, it is a sin. Forgive so you can be forgiven. There is no other way than the Word of God, and you have already seen it in Matthew 6:12.

I hope that as you read this portion, you have been examining your heart. So I ask you, what's in your cup—blessings or curses? I pray it is full of blessings, and if you do not see your blessings, stay with me as we examine the different cups from a biblical perspective. This God-given point of view will help you stand up and line up more firmly on solid ground with your Lord Jesus Christ.

Years ago, the Holy Spirit ministered to a young lady who had been abused as a wife. The marriage lasted only three and a half years, but it seemed to her to last an eternity. She was beat up, as she liked to say, for breakfast, lunch, dinner, and snacks. Many times, she was beat up so badly that she had to be taken to the hospital. Her coworkers would say things like, "He beat the living daylight out of you again last night." She was so embarrassed, and she felt trapped in that ungodly relationship. The man had never loved her. Unbeknownst to her, he had married her so he could come to the United States. She got it, and she gets it. After all, it is the land of opportunities; therefore, many want to come to the country. But what she could not understand was the abuse. She had to leave that toxic relationship if she wanted to stay alive. Finally, after three and a half years of that horrible life and many suicide attempts, she got the courage to leave him, and for seven consecutive years afterward, when she said the Lord's Prayer nightly, she would insert his name and verbally forgive him. To her surprise, they were just empty words. She never meant any of it. It wasn't until two years after she had dedicated her life to Jesus that the Holy Spirit asked her to pray for the man and she realized that she had never forgiven him. For two weeks straight, the Holy Spirit asked her to pray for him. She told the Holy Spirit repeatedly that there were many Christians in the world and He could use one of them to pray for him. She also asked the Holy Spirit if He did not know what the man had done to her.

Finally, she said to the Holy Spirit, "All right! I'll pray for him." She had to repent and ask the Holy Spirit to forgive her for her sour attitude. She was forgiven, and she went right into prayer for the man. What she did not know is that the Lord wanted to set her free from her past. It wasn't about him completely. It was about her heart and the purifying that she needed. Obedience is always better than sacrifice. She had sacrificed her wholeness for a long time, and her heavenly Father wanted her to be made free from all the pain and suffering that man had caused her.

Sometime later, she found out that the man had been in an accident on exactly the same day she had submitted to the Holy Spirit and prayed for him. His right wrist had been cut by some glass, and he had lost a lot of blood. He was hospitalized and lost the use of his right hand, and he could not work for an entire year. This she knew personally because she saw him at the end of the year, and he still was out of work and had the scars to prove the story was true. Did her prayers help him? Only God knows. All she knows is that because she was obedient to the voice of the Holy Spirit, she had been set free and could now talk about her story to help other battered wives because it does not hurt her anymore. She knows that she is free because of the grace and mercy of God in her life. She loves to say that she is blessed beyond measure because whoever the Son, Jesus Christ, makes free stays free indeed. "If the Son therefore shall make you free, you shall be free indeed" (John 8:36 KJV). She thanks her Lord and Savior Jesus Christ for the forgiveness, healing, and freedom found in the cup of the Lord.

— 3 —

The Voice in the Cup of the Lord vs. The Voice in the Cup of Demons

Scriptures clearly state that you must choose one cup or the other. "Ye cannot drink the cup of the Lord, and the cup of devils: ye cannot be partakers of the Lord's table, and the table of devils" (1 Cor. 10:21 KJV). You cannot drink from both cups. Truth be known, in the natural, it is impossible to drink from two cups at the same time. Put your straws away; you cannot use them in this scenario. One of the cups must be elevated while the other is lowered. If you try to drink from both cups at the same time, there will be some spillage and mixing, which are irreverent. I ask you to choose this day the Lord's cup, but before you do, if you have not already chosen the Lord's cup, consider the consequences of your choosing.

Looking at a cup again, it is an earthen container as you are an earthly vessel. When you drink from the cup that I invite you to drink from, that is, the cup of the Lord, it means you are partaking of the type of fellowship that Jesus offers.

Remember that you cannot serve two masters. "No man can serve two masters: for either he will hate the one and love the other; or else he will hold to the one and despise the other. Ye cannot serve God and mammon" (Matt. 6:24 KJV). You must let go of one and hold fast to the other. Jesus said that you cannot serve God and the spirit of mammon, or money.

Many in the United States suffer from this spirit of mammon. Nothing is good enough. They want bigger houses, more expensive cars, and full bank accounts. Some do not know how to live in faith, trusting God for their every need. The more they accumulate, the more they want. They have forgotten that they will leave this earth one day and everything will be left behind. They do not serve the Lord the way He ordained for their lives, because they must make more money so they can buy more stuff, and when they depart, someone most likely not deserving of their hard labor will inherit what they worked for and squander it all in no time at all. And when they stand before the Lord, they will be ashamed. Why not rebuke the spirit of mammon, cast it out of your life, and live for Jesus, fulfilling His every word in your life?

It wasn't too long after I gave my life to Christ Jesus that I asked Him what the most profitable business would be for me to go into. I was young and needed guidance, but I wanted from the Lord and not the world. To my surprise, He responded right away. He said, "The most profitable business for you to get into is the business of soul winning." I should have known that because that is the Father's heart, and that is what Jesus gave His life for. He came to seek and save the lost, and that is what He wants His followers to do. So I ask you, are you in the "right" business? Are you doing the Father's business, or are you doing your business?

You must treasure God's Word and hide it in your heart as you live for His glory. You are made of dust, and so you are a type of clay vessel, but in Jesus you can be a vessel of honor; while the treasure that you have is contained in the earthen vessel, you, in Jesus you can give God all the praise and glory due Him. He does not share His praise, nor does He share the glory belonging unto Him and Him alone. As an earthen vessel, you know that all you do is because of the benefits provided for you in His salvation. Let's examine what is in the Lord's cup of salvation, and then we will look at the cup of demons.

– 4 –

The Voice in the Cup of His Salvation

King David, a man after God's own heart, said, "I will take the cup of salvation, and call upon the name of the LORD" (Ps. 116:13 KJV). The cup of salvation contains all the blessings of God, especially those of eternal life and reward in God's kingdom. Some think that the kingdom of God is a far-distant and bizarre concept, while others believe it is just a myth. Regardless of what people belief, His kingdom is real, even more so than the earth He spoke into existence for us to live in. According to Jesus, heaven and earth will end, but God's Word will remain forever: "Heaven and earth shall pass away, but my words shall not pass away" (Matt. 24:35 KJV). You see, Jesus is the Word of God, and He already died for all. He lives forever. He will never die, and since He is the Word, the Word will never pass away. It will never die. You do not have to die either, and death is nothing more than being separated from God's presence. Choose life eternal and live forevermore with Jesus. "I am he that liveth and was dead; and, behold, I am alive forevermore, Amen; and have the keys of Hades and of death" (Rev. 1:18 KJV). Use your measure of faith and live!

To partake of the cup of salvation, you must have the faith to believe that it exists. God has given you a measure of faith. "For I say, through the grace given unto me, to every man that is among you, not to think of himself more highly than he ought to think; but to think soberly, according as God hath dealt to every man the measure of faith" (Rom. 12:3 KJV).

God is not asking you to believe in something He has not provided for, nor is He asking you to do it in your own strength.

He has given you a measure of faith to believe Him and His Word. Therefore, you must use the faith He has given you, for without faith you cannot please Him: "But without faith *it is* impossible to please *him*: for he that cometh to God must believe that he is, and *that* he is a rewarder of them that diligently seek him" (Heb. 11:6 KJV). This measure of faith given to believers can increase in you through reading, studying, and listening to the Word of God. This is how you study to show yourself approved unto God: you must actively engage in applying the Word of God in your life. You cannot be merely a speaker and not a doer of the Word. "Study to show thyself approved unto God, a workman that needeth not to be ashamed, rightly dividing the word of truth" (2 Tim. 2:15 KJV). There is something special about seeing the Word of God manifested in your life and the lives of those around you.

The Bible says that, by the word of two or three witnesses, a thing is established. I have given you more than three sources in the scriptures above. However, here is another scripture for further confirmation: "This *is* the third *time* I am coming to you. In the mouth of two or three witnesses shall every word be established" (2 Cor. 13:1 KJV).

What is in the cup of salvation? Before I tell you what's in it, let me tell you the price of this cup, for it is not cheap, nor are its contents discounted. Beginning in the book of Genesis, we see the first promise of the cup of salvation: "And I will put enmity between thee and the woman, and between thy seed and her seed; it shall bruise thy head, and thou shalt bruise his heel" (Gen. 3:15 KJV).

You are familiar with these words. At least, you know about Adam and Eve's sin of disobedience and how Satan tricked them into disobeying God. It is immediately after their act of disobedience that the Lord made the promise to redeem humankind back to Him. The first animal sacrifice is performed by God Himself: "Unto Adam also and his wife did the Lord God make coats of skins, and clothed them" (Gen. 3:21 KJV). And the last is performed by Him again, but this time, He is the sacrificial Lamb: "But this man, after he had offered one sacrifice for sins for ever, sat down on the right hand of God" (Heb. 10:12 KJV). Thus, it is the cup of His salvation from which you must drink if you want to become a child of God and inherit the kingdom of heaven. No one—I repeat, no one—will inherit the kingdom of heaven unless he or she drinks from this cup. "Jesus saith unto him, I am the way, the truth, and the life: no man cometh unto the Father, but by me" (John 14:6 KJV).

So what's in this cup? Let's look at what Jesus put in the cup so you can drink freely from it. You have heard stories and fables about the cup of the Lord. Let us examine the truth of the matter.

Jesus Christ is the same yesterday, today, and forever. He is the alpha and omega, the beginning and the end. He is the King of Kings and the Lord of Lords. He is the Word of God. The fact of the matter is that Jesus is God Himself, who stripped Himself of all His glory to come to earth to be born of a woman—the virgin Mary, His earth mother, God's chosen vessel. Make no mistake, though: He is God.

> In the beginning was the Word, and the Word was with God, and the Word was God. The same was in the beginning with God. All things were made by him; and without him was not anything made that was made. In him was life; and the life was the light of men. And the light shineth in darkness; and the darkness

comprehended it not.... [That] was the true Light, which lighteth every man that cometh into the world. He was in the world, and the world was made by him, and the world knew him not. He came unto his own, and his own received him not. But as many as received him, to them gave He, power to become the sons of God, [even] to them that believe on his name: Which were born, not of blood, nor of the will of the flesh, nor of the will of man, but of God. (John 1:1–5, 10–13 KJV).

Jesus is the Light of mankind. Without Him, we live in darkness and have the expected end of eternal damnation. Thus, He came and paid the great price for us. Was stripping Himself of His majesty not enough? He had to be the sacrificial Lamb required by God for our sin, for the wages of sin is death. We all deserve death and eternal punishment, but—thank God for His mercy—He made a way. To have a better understanding of this awesome cup, which is our blessing, let's look at hell for a moment.

You must understand why He had to pay with His own life to purchase your life. Hell, as described by the Word of God, is not a pretty place, nor was it created for God's people, whom He created in His own image. Hell was created for Satan and his demons.

Take a closer look at this awful place according to God's description, not that of Hollywood or some other ill-informed sources. As you look at scriptures, you will see that hell is a place of everlasting burning with an unquenchable fire. It is a place of torment where worms do not die and continuously feast on those residing there. The other important thing to look at and meditate on is the fact that, once one enters hell, there is no way out. It is here on earth that you make the decision to serve God the Father, God the Son, and God the Holy Spirit. Unlike some believe, there is no purgatory, no holding place for the dead. Therefore, you cannot pray people out of a nonexistent place. That is deception from Satan to keep you ignorant and, in the end, have you and those who believed his lies to end up in hell with him.

Obviously, Satan does not want to have an empty kingdom of hell, and he desires to take as many as he can with him. Once there, he will torment his residents as he will be tormented himself forever. Remember, hell is not for you; it is for Satan and his demons. Jesus has made a way of escape. All you must do is repent, believe in your heart, and confess with your mouth, thus accepting Him as your Lord and Savior. It is that simple. It is a gift, the gift of salvation contained in His cup for you and for me. You do not have to work for it as some people believe. It is given by grace and not by works; otherwise, people would boast about their own salvation. Yes, you do work after you have been saved because you love your Lord. He first loved you and gave His life for you. You also labor because you learned about the truth concerning hell, and you do not want anyone to end up in that awful place for a second, never mind an eternity. Eternity never ends; hence, the pain of hell will never end. You work out of love and not to purchase your salvation. Jesus did that for you.

I am sure you have heard of people who are afraid of dying, and here is the reason for the fear: "The sinners in Zion are afraid; fearfulness hath surprised the hypocrites. Who among us shall dwell with the devouring fire? Who among us shall dwell with everlasting burnings?" (Isa. 33:14 KJV).

There comes a time when you must face facts, a time when you no longer play the ignorant card. It is a game that you cannot win, and there is too much at stake. I dare not gamble with my life, eternal life. I have heard people say, "I have time," but time is not guaranteed to any of us. Yes! Count the cost of serving the Lord, but I guarantee that you will find no one else who will reward you for your diligence better than Jesus. Don't take my word for it, though; find out for yourself. I encourage you to seize the moment and make things right with God, if you have not done so, right now. Just say, "Lord, Jesus, I repent from all my sins and ask you to forgive me and come into my life. Lord, be my Savior, my healer and my deliverer. Be my all in all."

Satan loves it when you so ignorantly make unwise statements and decisions because he knows that he has you at that moment. That is when he does his best to take you out. I have heard some say that they will attend God's house when they get their act together. That is another one of Satan's tricks. He will make sure you never get your life together. Besides, isn't that the job of the Holy Spirit—to guide and lead you in Christ? You cannot do it without the Spirit of the living God. To think that you can is deception, and Satan is the master of deception. "Whose fan *is* in his hand, and he will thoroughly purge his floor, and gather his wheat into the garner; but he will burn up the chaff with unquenchable fire" (Matt. 3:12 KJV).

Others say they must work. Their jobs have become their God. Yes, people must work. The Bible says that those who do not work do not eat. But everything has a balance. Give God His time first. Make your time spent with Him the first priority in your daily routine, and you will see that He will bless you so that you do not have to work as hard. God blesses those who honor Him. Honor God with your all, and He will not disappoint you. Believe in His Son and you have believed in Him. If you do not believe in His Son, Jesus Christ, you make Him to be a liar, and there is no salvation for you. Also, as you live for Christ, make sure all you do is for His glory and not yours. If you work with unclean hands and an impure heart, your work and even you may burn. "And these shall go away into everlasting punishment: but the righteous into life eternal" (Matt. 25:46 KJV). You must keep a sincere heart before God and humans. You have nothing to prove to people, but you will give an account to God. "And shall cast them into a furnace of fire: there shall be wailing and gnashing of teeth" (Matt. 13:42 KJV). "Then shall he say also unto them on the left hand, Depart from me, ye cursed, into everlasting fire, prepared for the devil and his angels" (Matt. 25:41 KJV). As you read these last scriptures, I pray you realized how precious salvation is and that you have already drank from the cup of His salvation, even before we have looked at the price He paid for it.

Jesus came, and the people did not recognize Him as the Savior of the world. Satan thought he had Him, but he was mistaken. The plan of God was too good to be derailed. Satan thought he was punishing Jesus, but in fact he was right in the middle of God's plan. Had he known the plan of God, the plan of salvation, he would not have rejoiced in Jesus's suffering for you before the cross and on the cross. In the cup of Salvation, you find Jesus's suffering. His cup of salvation for you is the cup of suffering for Him. In Jesus's cup of salvation are your blessings and mine. Jesus paid a full price for those who believe. He paid for our spiritual death, infirmity, poverty, sickness, and diseases with His life. In Jesus, we have eternal life through salvation; we have healing, deliverance, and provision for all our needs.

> Who hath believed our report? and to whom
> is the arm of the LORD revealed? For he shall
> grow up before him as a tender plant, and as
> a root out of a dry ground: he hath no form
> nor comeliness; and when we shall see him,
> [there is] no beauty that we should desire him.
> He is despised and rejected of men; a man of
> sorrows, and acquainted with grief: and we
> hid as it were [our] faces from him; he was
> despised, and we esteemed him not. Surely he
> hath borne our griefs, and carried our sorrows:
> yet we did esteem him stricken, smitten of

God, and afflicted. But he [was] wounded for our transgressions, [he was] bruised for our iniquities: the chastisement of our peace [was] upon him; and with his stripes we are healed. All we like sheep have gone astray; we have turned everyone to his own way; and the LORD hath laid on him the iniquity of us all. He was oppressed, and he was afflicted, yet he opened not his mouth: he is brought as a lamb to the slaughter, and as a sheep before her shearers is dumb, so he openeth not his mouth. (Isa. 53:1–7 KJV).

As you read the scriptures above, you can't help but examine each point in His suffering. So many have labeled you and have put a value of nothing on you. Some have negotiated your worth not knowing that there is no price for which you can be bought because you were already purchased with a great price, and that is the life of Jesus Christ your Savior. I know my worth. Do you know yours?

The next time someone tries to sell you out for cheap, remind them of your worth in Jesus. There are no dowries that represent your value to Christ and to God. Tell them to keep their cows and their goats. Tell them to keep their cheap dinners and ninety-nine-cent bars of soap! Tell them that toilet paper is for the bathroom and the rag for the kitchen floor! Take down the for-sale sign and tell them you are not for sale. The Prince of Peace has your heart in His, and that is where you are staying, untouchable and unmovable, because that is where you belong. You belong in His chamber of love, His Holy of Holies, and when He looks at you, He sees His shed blood for you, and the mercy seat cries out on your behalf. So stand strong and do not compromise with the enemy of your body, soul, and spirit. You will not romance or sleep with the enemy. You are the body of Christ, the bride of Christ, and the temple of His Holy Spirit. You are faithful, and you honor your Bridegroom.

I remember vaguely the pain of molestation but not the physical aspect of it; rather, I recall the words that were spoken:" I touched you, but it was intended for your sister." These awful words echoed through time and space. Well, molester, I wasn't even good enough to be molested? Those were the words Satan whispered in my ear from time to time until I rebuked him in the name of Jesus, and I was made free.

How many have hurt you and made you feel that you were not even good enough to be hurt? That is the lie that Satan, who is the father of lies, tells to keep you in bondage, but I thank my Jesus for His delivering power. When He took on the crown of thorns, it was for things like the healing of the mind and bad memories. I do not have to relive the past. And you do not have to relive the past either. I remember a young lady to whom the Holy Spirit ministered years ago who had been repeatedly raped and physically and emotionally abused terribly. Her parents were good people but could not really help her much because they were new in the country and had limited English proficiency at that time. But do you know what? Jesus set her free. She was left with scars that she did not think would ever heal, but Jesus paid for them also. By His stripes she has been healed, and so are you, if only you believe. "Who his own self bear our sins in his own body on the tree, that we, being dead to sins, should live unto righteousness: by whose stripes ye were healed" (1 Peter 2:24 KJV). This scripture is one that I shared with the young lady.

I have ownership of this scripture. I know it works. It worked for her, it works for me, and it will work for you. God is no respecter of persons; He does not discriminate. All you must do is believe Him and take Him at His Word. As you look at the suffering of Jesus, let's look at it from a love standpoint. Every insult, every spitting on His face, and every nail He took, as well as the piercing of His side and His unrecognizable state, was for you. He did it for you. Keep in mind that He was sinless. The punishment He took before and during the cross was for you. You are the sinner, not Him. A love like that deserves your undivided attention. Don't you ever forget it or take it for granted. One way you can honor the cross of Christ is by living the life He purchased for you daily—neglecting nothing, taking nothing for granted, but with thanksgiving living for Him and working for His kingdom of heaven.

Are you ready to drink from His cup of salvation? Come on! Taste and see that the Lord is good. "O taste and see that the Lord is good: blessed is the man that trusts him" (Ps. 34:8 KJV). I hear you. You said you already drank from the cup, but don't you know this is a daily activity, a lifestyle? You cannot take only one sip and think that you are okay. You must come into fellowship with Jesus daily to maintain the intimate relationships He so desires with you. Communion with the Lord is vitally important to a great relationship with the Father, Son, and Holy Spirit. Remember, those who do not drink from His cup of salvation or blessings will drink from the cup of demons. You cannot drink from both cups. You must choose daily whose cup is your drinking cup. King David chose the Lord's cup. First, he said that he shall not live in want. "The Lord is my Shepherd; I shall not want" (Ps. 23:1 KJV). Imagine having all your needs and even your wants met, desiring nothing, because you have it all. That is why King David could say that his cup runneth over. He had blessings upon blessings. He lived an abundant life, lacking in no area. He did not spent time worrying about his provision. He had time to worship his God. "Thou preparest a table before me in the presence of mine enemies; thou anointed my head with oil; my cup runneth over" (Ps. 23:5 KJV). Like King David, I choose the Lord's cup. How about you?

When I say *choose*, I am not just talking to unbelievers; I am talking to believers also. Some believe that they can live in the world and in the House of the Lord. Not so. Wake up! Think of the Church of Laodicea—lukewarm. Those who are lukewarm stand the danger of being spewed out of Jesus's mouth. He desires that you be hot in passionate love and commitment to Him; but if not, then be cold. He can work with you when you are cold. He can revive you, but when you think you are okay and you do not need or want God's help, you are in big trouble. You adopt an unteachable spirit, and nothing can be done for you. In this state, you lie to yourself. The prophet Isaiah said to not hide from your own flesh.

"Is it not to share your bread with the hungry, And that you bring to your house the poor who are cast out; When you see the naked, that you cover him, And not hide yourself from your own flesh?" (Isa. 58:7 KJV). I get what the prophet was saying. I live with transparency to self and others.

God is omniscient, and nothing escapes Him. So why not just admit that you have a problem and deal with it as soon as it arises? Pride comes before a fall. Pride is dangerous to you and to those with whom you associate. I normally begin my prayers with a petition to the Holy Spirit to show me myself. Once He does, I repent and ask for forgiveness right there and then. I want to be in right standing with Him always. There is no reason to try to conceal things from the Lord, who is all knowing. I bare myself before Him, and you should do the same. He already knows everything about you, so if you conceal things, you hide them from yourself and not from Him or from others. Nothing hidden stays hidden. Sooner or later, it will come to light. Therefore, tell God everything so that your flesh can have peace! Be still. Tell it that you will not hear its voice. Do like Jesus did with the storm. Calm it right down. "And he arose and rebuked the wind, and said unto the sea, Peace, be still. And the wind ceased, and there was a great calm" (Mark 4:39 KJV).

Let me pause here to tell you about a secret, or so I thought. I started attending a church, and as soon as I walked in the doors, the very first day, the Lord revealed to me that the lady, I will call her Marta, who was the ladies' ministry leader, was a smoker. I admit that I disrespectfully said to the Lord, 'What is that to me?' I repented later, and I understood that at that time, He just wanted me to pray for Marta's deliverance. Now, Marta was so clean that unless the Holy Spirit revealed it to you, you would never know she was a smoker by her clothes or anything else. Later, she and I became prayer partners, and we would pray every Sunday for an hour for the Sunday service. One fine Sunday morning, the Holy Spirit told me to pray for her three times. Three times, I told the Holy Spirit that Marta was not ready. And as you can imagine, I did not pray for her. I know I was disobedient, but thanks be to God for His mercy. The service was over, and I went home. Not too long after I got home, the phone rang. It was Marta. She said to me, "Benedita, the Lord told me to tell you that I am ready." I said to her, "Well, if you are ready, I will pray for you on Wednesday when we have our women's meeting." I was still on my high horse, right? Yes. After I hung up the telephone, I was so upset. I kept telling the Holy Spirit as if it was His fault. *I can't believe you told on me, Holy Spirit. Holy Spirit You told on me. I tell you the truth, thank God for His mercy.* I did pray for the lady as agreed, and Jesus set her free from the nicotine spirit of addition. Her husband said that he had to be set free too, and he became free that next Sunday. Why have I said all this? I tell you this to let you know there are no secrets, and I am transparent in my delivery. I tell you my shortcomings and show you the mercy of God that is fresh and new every day. Today, I do my very best to obey Him as quickly as He speaks to me. You need to know that there are no secrets. God knows it all, and He does reveal it to others. Just because they are not at liberty to say, it does not mean that no one knows your hidden sins.

If you think that no one knows, you are deceiving yourself and only yourself.

Secret sins are dangerous, and they will put you in a dangerous zone. This lukewarm state is where you do the most damage to yourself and to the kingdom of God. You do not enter in, nor do you let those who desire to enter in enter. In this place of complacency is where you act as the brood of vipers Jesus was talking about. Unless you change your mind-set, heart, and life, you stand the chance of hellfire, as already described. You do not want that. Please put your pride aside. Better yet, ask God, the Holy Spirit, to set you free from this spirit, the spirit of pride or the Leviathan spirit. Only the Holy Spirit of the Living God can and will turn your heart toward home to Jesus. Pick up your cross daily and follow Jesus. God is sovereign, and He does not lie. Believe His Word when He says there is a punishment and hell for the wicked. I am a firm believer that if you do not drink from the cup of the Lord's suffering, then you will not drink from the cup of His blessings. So drink up! The cup of blessing is yours for the receiving and the drinking. Feast on and live!

— 5 —

Blessings in the Cup of the Lord

There are many blessings in the cup of the Lord, but we will examine just a few of them to give you a taste for more. I will start with the voice in the cup that cries out on your behalf for the remission of your sins: "For this is My blood of the new covenant, which is shed for many for the remission of sins" (Matt. 26:28 KJV). With an understanding of this scripture, you know that Jesus paid with His blood the price required by God for sins. Because of His sacrifice, you have been exempted from the consequences of your wrongdoing and forgiven; therefore, you do not have to suffer the penalty of death and hellfire.

Jesus's sacrifice has provided life that is abundant life for those who partake of His flesh and of His blood. "Then Jesus said to them, 'Most assuredly, I say to you, unless you eat the flesh of the Son of Man and drink His blood, you have no life in you'" (John 6:53 NKJV). Some had problems with this because they did not understand what Jesus was telling them. You cannot understand spiritual things with the natural mind. You must solicit the help of the Holy Spirit if you want to comprehend spiritual matters. The only way you abide in Christ is by becoming one with Him just as He is one with the Father. Communion with Jesus causes you to dwell in Him and Him in you. "He who eats My flesh and drinks My blood abides in Me, and I in him" (John 6:56 NKJV).

The blood of Jesus also purchased the church. Some think that the church is a building, but they are mistaken. We Christians, collectively, are the body of Christ and the church, the universal church. You must be careful to not handle God's people wrongly. After all, He paid a great price for them as well. "Take heed therefore, unto yourselves, and to all the flock, over the which the Holy Ghost hath made you overseers, to feed the church of God, which He hath purchased with His own blood" (Acts 20:28 KJV).

Through His shed blood, Jesus became your atonement through faith. Jesus took the punishment due you on Himself, so you do not have to suffer for your transgression. Jesus, the amazing Savior bore it all on the cross of Calvary. There is no sin too great, and there are no sins left unpaid. It is Jesus's sacrifice that paid for it all, and once and for all. He, Jesus is the one, "Who God set forth as propitiation by His blood, through faith, to demonstrate His righteousness, because in His forbearance God passed over the sins that were previously committed" (Rom. 3:25 NKJV).

Jesus justified you and saved you from the cup of the fierce anger and wrath of God through His obedience to God in becoming the sacrificial Lamb for humankind. He took your place on the cross, saving you from the punishment due you. "Much more then, having now been justified by His blood, we shall be saved from wrath through Him" (Rom. 5:9 KJV).

Jesus redeemed you knowing that you were not redeemed by corruptible things, such as silver or gold, from your adrift conduct passed down by tradition from your forebears but with the precious blood of Christ, as of a lamb without blemish and without spot. In Him, we have redemption through His blood, the forgiveness of sins, according to the riches of His grace (Eph. 1:7, 1 Peter 1:18–19 KJV). There is a song sung in heaven to honor Jesus for redeeming you back to your Father God. (Rev. 5:9–14 KJV).

Jesus's blood is presented in heaven, and it is on the mercy seat where the Father can look at it. The blood cries out for mercy day and night for you. The blood speaks on your behalf, and because of it, you can come boldly to the throne of grace in Jesus's name and make your petitions known to the Father. You do not need a priest or a preacher to speak on your behalf because the blood of Jesus does it for you. This does not mean that you should not ask for prayer, for it is scriptural to seek prayer of the elders of the church and to pray one for another. I am referring to those who do not pray for themselves thinking that it is forbidden of them or that they are not good enough to talk to Father God. That is not true. The blood makes you righteous in Jesus's name before Him. God wants to communicate with you. He loves you and wants to fellowship with you daily. Please ask for prayer; but pray for yourself also. Pray with confidence in the blood of Jesus. It was shed for you. After you have finished praying, sing with the angels a new song unto the Lord for what He has done for you. Worship Him in spirit and in truth. The Father seeks those who will worship Him with sincerity of heart. "And they sang a new song, saying: 'You are worthy to take the scroll, and to open its seals; For You were slain, and have redeemed us to God by Your blood out of every tribe and tongue and people and nation'" (Rev. 5:9 NKJV).

The blood of Jesus has brought you who were far away from God near to Him. Sin separated you from the Holy God. Your sins kept you at a great distance from your Father God, but the precious blood of Jesus has brought you close to Him. You do not have to fear God. The cost of your sins has been paid for by the blood of His Son, Jesus Christ. But now in Christ Jesus, you who once were far off have been brought near by the blood of Christ (Eph. 2:13 NKJV). Jesus made a way for you to commune with the Father. You can now sit on your Daddy's lap, lean on His bosom, and gaze into His loveliness. You can gaze into His eyes, the eyes of your heavenly Father, without distress and without dread. He is love, and He loves you. "For God so loved the world that

He gave His only begotten Son, that whoever believes in Him should not perish but have everlasting life" (John 3:16 NKJV).

This is God's desire for the world. How much more for those who have accepted His Son as Lord and Savior? No, brother; no, sister—fear not. God is good to His sons and daughters. He sent Jesus to redeem you back to Him. You are a part of the family of God through Jesus. Through Jesus's blood you have the forgiveness of sins in which you have redemption. You are made new, and you are a new creature by the power of Jesus's blood. "Who hath delivered us from the power of darkness and hath translated us into the kingdom of his dear Son: In whom we have redemption through His blood, even the forgiveness of sins (Col. 1:13–14 KJV).

Jesus's blood brought you peace, a peace that you cannot comprehend. It is in Jesus, the Prince of Peace, and in His blood that you have been reconciled back to your God and King. In peace there is no horror, and you benefit from the peace that surpasses all understanding because of the blood of Christ Jesus. "And by Him to reconcile all things to Himself, by Him, whether things on earth or things in heaven, having made peace through the blood of His cross" (Col. 1:20 NKJV).

I know the blood works. It wasn't too long ago that I was in a foreign country, trying to rest after a long day. The culture called for sleeping on the floor, and it was late in the afternoon when I decided to take a nap before dinner. I was harassed by demons the entire time, so I decided to get up, wash up, and go to dinner. Nighttime was no different. I was awakened many times during the night. The demons were not pleased with my being there. They decided to torment me by trying to lie down on top of me, choking me, and doing any other activities they could conjure up. Each time, I was awakened by their harassments; I pled the blood of Jesus. They had to leave. I finally said to them, "Keep coming back and disturbing my sleep. All you are doing is giving me opportunities to plead the blood of Jesus Christ and claim this land for Father God in Jesus's name." I was at a high place where demons were worshiped, and after I said that, I had no problem sleeping the rest of the time I was there.

I wonder sometimes why God takes me to these places, but I do not question His sovereignty. The blood works. You must know that it works for you. Satan and his demons are afraid of the blood of Jesus because they know they were defeated at the cross by the shed blood of Jesus Christ for your sins. Pleading the blood of Jesus against them leaves them powerless in your life because the blood protects you from all their attacks. I chose to partake from the cup of the Lord's blessing. How about you?

The cup of demons is for demons and not for you.

– 6 –

The Voice in the Cup of Demons

Have you made a conscious decision to reject the cup of this world, the cup of demons of Babylon, and embrace the cup of the Lord? As you have already seen, you cannot drink from these two cups, and God will not mix them; they are totally unharmonious. You must choose one or the other. As the apostle Paul said, "We cannot drink of the Lord's cup and of the cup of demons" (1 Cor. 10:21 NKJV). You must totally reject this world, this Babylon, and that awful cup of the false church, full of her abominations and of the blood of the saints. "Reward her even as she rewarded you, and double unto her double according to her works: in the cup which she hath filled fill to her double" (Rev. 18:6 KJV).

Life is in the blood. Demons are spirits and do not have blood, nor can they produce blood. You have already seen the importance of the human blood. Satan and his demons try to have a counterfeit for everything God has and does. Since they cannot produce or reproduce blood, they seek to take advantage of the blood of the innocent for their evil deeds. Because demons are spirits, they need bodies to function here on earth, so they find willing and unwilling hosts to carry them. These are the ones who are possessed, oppressed, depressed, and obsessed. They are under Satan's control and will do whatever he demands of them. Many wonder why things are happening in the manner that they are. This is a fallen world, and the enemy is at his best doing his worst.

Thank God for His people and for His Holy Spirit who are still here on earth, but remove the two and it is darkness to the maximum, a darkness that is inconceivable. At this point, I am reminded of the man with the legion. What did he do? Or was he just at the wrong place at the wrong time? Regardless of his situation or location, he drank from the cup of demons for a while.

"And he said, Legion: because many devils were entered into him" (Luke 8:30 KJV). He was so bound that he could not be around people and lived in a cemetery. This poor man carried thousands of demons. But one fine day, Jesus came by and set him free. The demons spoke to Jesus and asked Him why He had come before their time to torment them, and they asked Jesus to send them into a herd of pigs that was feeding on the mountainside. Jesus permitted it, but the amazing thing is that even the pigs refused to carry demons. How much more should you, created in God's image, refuse to host demons? It's sad to say, but some do not. Satan has promised them things he has no intention of delivering, thus filling their cups with demonic and poisonous venom that they will have to drink if they do not repent from their wicked ways. So what's in the cup of demons?

We have already established that demons do not have blood because they are spirits. In the cup of demons is found the blood of the innocent, stolen goods, lies, the wine of immorality, the lust of fornication and adultery, deception, and all that is perverted. This is the abominable cup. This cup is filled with all that is detestable and against God. Those who partake of it will have to partake of the cup of God's wrath. Just as you drink from the Lord's cup of suffering, you will drink from His cup of salvation and blessings. And if you refuse, you will drink from the cup of demons. Then, you will drink from the cup of the wrath of God. No evil deed will go unpunished. Those who serve Satan and his demons think they are special or have special powers, but what they have is limited and temporary power. Why not follow and serve the omnipotent One and drink from the cup of the Lord?

Satan tried with the man Jesus too. He tried to get Jesus to fall for his trap, but Jesus, filled with the Holy Spirit, did not need any more power than what He already possessed. How about you? Are you filled with the Holy Spirit? He is the power of God here on earth with us and within us. Have you believed the lie and rejected the Holy Spirit's baptism? This is one of Satan's lies. He tries to keep people far from the baptism of the Holy Spirit with lies because he knows that once you have a relationship with the Spirit of the living God, you will have nothing to do with him. In fact, he becomes powerless in your life because the Holy Spirit will reveal the truth about him, which will expel all the lies he has told you and others around you. After all, Satan is a liar and the father of lies. He could not tell the truth even if he tried, which he will not. So don't believe his lies. "Ye are of *your* father the devil, and the lusts of your father ye will do. He was a murderer from the beginning, and abode not in the truth, because there is no truth in him. When he speaketh a lie, he speaketh of his own: for he is a liar, and the father of it" (John 8:44 KJV). Refrain from drinking from the cup of demons. It is full of detestable things, and the result is damnation."

"Know ye not that the unrighteous shall not inherit the kingdom of God? Be not deceived: neither fornicators, nor idolaters, nor adulterers, nor effeminate, nor abusers of themselves with mankind" (1 Cor. 6:9 KJV).

Many deceivers have come into the world saying that anything goes, but again, that is deception and belongs in the cup of demons. "For many deceivers are entered into the world, who confess not that Jesus Christ is come in the flesh. This is a deceiver and an anti-Christ (2 John 2:7 KJV). This spirit of anti-Christ will tell you to do what feels good, but you know that this walk is not about feelings. Feelings come from the flesh, and flesh will not inherit the kingdom of heaven, so it does not care. Do not cater to flesh but to the spirit of man, who is eternal. You are created in God's image, and since He is eternal, that makes you eternal as well.

Why am I saying this? I need you to understand that there is an "after-earth" that is more real that this present state you find yourself in. Earth is temporary, but heaven is eternal, and so is hell. Keep yourself away from the cup of demons, and take hold with a strong grip of the cup of the Lord Jesus Christ. Drink of it and enjoy it! It was provided for you and for me. If you reject the cup of the Lord, you will drink from the cup of God's wrath. Pray right now and ask the Lord to help you drink from His cup. Sometimes, all you have to say is, "Jesus help me," and immediately, He will be in the scene.

— 7 —

The Voice in the Cup of the Fierce Anger and the Wrath of God

I want to start by saying that the cup of God's wrath is for Satan, his demons, and those who utterly reject the cup of the Lord. Do not take this lightly. It is vitally important that you pay close attention to this teaching. It can save your life and those of people to whom you teach the Word of God. Do not compromise with the enemy. Satan is a liar and a deceiver. He can paint beautiful pictures at times to entice you and to deceive you into thinking that he is the good guy. However, the Word of God is clear about who he is, and it is important that you understand that God has made every provision for you to live your eternal life in paradise with Him. Again, all you must do is accept His gift of life and drink from the cup of the Lord. Drink from the Lord's cup, and you are saved. Reject the cup of the Lord, and you are damned. "And whosoever was not found written in the book of life was cast into the lake of fire" (Rev. 20:15 KJV).

Everyone must accept the Lord Jesus as his or her Lord and Savior. Rejecting Jesus is a terrible decision. It is not a mistake, and it is not an error. It is a one-way ticket to hell. Those who refuse Jesus will have this fate as per the following scriptures:

> The same shall drink of the wine of the wrath of God, which is poured out without mixture into the cup of his indignation; and he shall be tormented with fire and brimstone in the presence of the holy angels, and in the presence of the Lamb: And the smoke of their torment ascendeth up for ever and ever: and they have no rest day nor night who worship the beast and his image, and whosoever receiveth the mark of his name. (Rev. 14:10–11 NKJV)

Do not be deceived into thinking that God does not mean what He says in His Word. He does. So do yourself a big favor, a favor of a lifetime—that is, eternal lifetime—and accept Jesus right now as your Lord and Savior. Take a break right here. Pick up the cup of salvation and enjoy a drink from it right now if you have not done so yet.

I am glad you did not provoke God to anger by rejecting His invitation. Those who do and continue serving their idols or demons stand in the way of their salvation and deliverance, and God is not pleased with them. "In that ye provoke me unto wrath with the works of your hands, burning incense unto other gods in the land of Egypt, whither ye be gone to dwell, that ye might cut yourselves off, and that ye might be a curse and a reproach among all the nations of the earth?" (Jer. 44:8 KJV). Let me take a minute to expound on this scripture. For example, suppose that one day, I decide to go out and pick a tree to have cut down. After it has been cut, I choose a piece of it—the best piece—and ask a friend who is skilled in woodwork to carve me a god or an idol. As for the rest of the tree I have cut, I use it to burn in my fireplace to keep me warm. The idol came from the same tree. Part of it I burn, and the other part I worship. Is there power in it to save me? Where does its power come from—the tree that is dead wood now, or demons who make sure there is just a little something going on to keep me interested and in bondage? Demons! How stupid is this? Yet many blinded by the enemy do it daily. I have witnessed people taking food to a tree and leaving it there as an offering while their children are going hungry. The tree does not move to receive it, nor does it eat the food. And left there for many days, the food will go bad. This is fact and not fiction.

Another thing that I have observed is the offering of fresh-cooked, delicious, choice cuts of meat to idols. A man carried a tray with freshly roasted pork; he entered a temple, took the best piece, offered it to the idol made of porcelain, and asked the idol to bless it for him and for his family. How does a deaf and dumb idol bless? It does not hear, it does not speak, nor does it move unless it is moved by demons. They do not possess the power to bless; rather, they have the power to curse. Immediately after his act, he left the temple with the remaining portion to feed his family. The meat was not blessed. It was cursed.

Demons do not bless; they curse. And this action brings the anger of God upon the lives of those who choose to engage in this type of service and of worship that is demonic. "And he shall say, Where are their gods, their rock in whom they trusted, which did eat the fat of their sacrifices and drank the wine of their drink offerings? Let them rise up and help you and be your protection" (Deut. 32:37–38 KJV).

You may be thinking that I am very critical. Rather, I am one who has been made free from the lies, deception, and bondage of Satan. Remember the young lady, Marta, who married a man who abused her? He also, unbeknownst to her, was involved in witchcraft. He thought that he was in control. In fact, he thought he could control his "gifts," but I am here to tell you that he was and is deceived. Satan never delivers what he promises. This man's life has been nothing but turmoil. I pray he gets set free from the paws of Satan before it is too late for him and for his new family. I encouraged Marta to pray for his deliverance, and I have prayed for him as well. Although he does deserve hell for what he has done to so many, Marta and I have prayed God's mercy on his life. Jesus died for him too.

Witchcraft is another way Satan keeps people in bondage. He harvests their God-given gifts and uses them to do his evil. Satan has no gifts for you. He does, however, counterfeit everything God has created. Divination is a counterfeit to the prophetic. You did not know or did not value the precious gift of prophecy God gave you, so Satan has deceived you into thinking that he has gifted you with the power of divination. Counterfeit! Look to God to meet your every need. He loves you and will forgive you of all your wrongdoing. He will not hold grudges. He will set you free and give you the gift of eternal life through His Son, Jesus Christ the Savior.

Don't provoke Him to anger. It will not go well for you. Take a moment and make the decision that is the best you will ever make. Turn to God and make peace with Him. He will not turn you away. You still have time, and now is the hour of salvation. Know that God will not share you with Satan for He is a jealous God. Make the commitment to serve God and God alone. "And what concord hath Christ with Belial? Or what part hath he that believeth with an infidel? And what agreement hath the temple of God with idols? For ye are the temple of the living God; as God hath said, I will dwell in them, and walk in them; and I will be their God, and they shall be my people. Wherefore come out from among them, and be ye separate, saith the Lord, and touch not the unclean thing; and I will receive you" (2 Cor. 6:15–17 KJV).

Do you hear the voice of God calling you to Him? God does not want you to be deceived, and He has provided His Word for you to be enlightened. You are the temple of His Holy Spirit. Satan tries again with the counterfeit to possess individuals, but he is trespassing on God's property. Don't let him use you as his host. Live for God, and let God live in you. You are the temple of His Holy Spirit. I gently and firmly ask you to drink from the cup of the Lord. Then, you will not have to drink from the cup of God's wrath.

I remember preaching years ago on this topic. A young man who was present rejected the message and was exposed right then and there for what he was doing. Had he embraced the Word and repented, he would not have been exposed. He became angry at the messenger. Unbeknownst to me in the natural, he had been partaking of two cups—the Lord's and the demons'. At least, it seemed that way at the time. But, as you have seen in this study, one cannot partake of both cups. That leaves us to think that he was deceived in thinking that he could partake of both. Well, I found God to be very merciful in His delivery, but the young man did not receive. He was very angry and left the church, but not before causing chaos. I pray that, wherever he is at this time, he has come to his senses and has been set free from that python spirit.

The python spirit comes against the Spirit of the living God as if he can win. It starts slowly, but it is precise and consistent with its deeds. It tries to squeeze the breath out of a person slowly but surely. This is how many have backslidden and without even realizing what was happening. They are put into a slumber state, and before too long, they are lukewarm, and Jesus finds them repugnant. You must be vigilant and pray against this spirit of divination and devastation. "And it came to pass, as we went to prayer, a certain damsel possessed with a spirit of divination met us, which brought her masters much gain by soothsaying" (Acts 16:16 KJV). This spirit is very charismatic in nature and can only be discerned by the gift of discerning of spirits. It comes against the Spirit of the living God in you in a very subtle way. It is very elusive in manner and in action. You must guard against it, and you must teach others concerning its subtleties.

The young man I referred to earlier was a registered sex offender. Had he repented when the Holy Spirit exposed Him in a subtle way and resigned from the youth leader position, he would not have been exposed in the manner that ended up happening. God always gives us opportunities to repent and make things right with Him and with others, but if we reject that opportunity in thinking that it is our secret and nobody knows nor will find out, we will be exposed. God will protect the innocent, and He does this for our benefit. Repentance is powerful, and we must take advantage of it. It's sad to say that many are too prideful to accept God's mercy. Don't let that be you.

Christians do not have to fear this spirit or harassing spirits. We have made the decision to partake of the Lord's cup, and in His cup of blessing is everything we need to fight the enemy. "Take counsel together, and it shall come to nought; speak the word, and it shall not stand: for God is with us" (Isa. 8:10 KJV). We know that God is with us, and if God is for us who can be against us? We live lives of love and of power. God has equipped us in every area of our lives. We have the name above all names, the name of Jesus. We have the powerful blood of Jesus, and we have the Holy Spirit of the living God here with us teaching us, training us, and staying with us through whatever tasks the Lord has set before us. We have God's Holy Bible for instruction, and we have been equipped by the living Word Himself. We fear nothing for we abide in love, and there is no fear in love. "There is no fear in love; but perfect love casteth out fear: because fear hath torment. He that feareth is not made perfect in love" (1 John 4:18 KJV). If you are connected to God's Love, you do not have to fear the cup of God's fierce anger and wrath. That is reserved for Satan and his demons. "Therefore, shall the Lord, the Lord of hosts, send among his fat ones leanness; and under his glory he shall kindle a burning like the burning of a fire" (Isa. 10:16 KJV).

Each morning, you wake up to a new day with new mercies. You must hold onto God's promises without wavering. You do not change, nor do you stand between two opinions. In other words, you do not drink from two different cups. You stay drinking from the fountain of life, which is found in the cup of the Lord. You follow God and God alone. "And Elijah came unto all the people, and said, How long halt ye between two opinions? If the LORD be God, follow him: but if Baal, then follow him. And the people answered him not a word" (1 Kings 18:21 KJV). In this scripture, God's people were a bit confused, but you know that confusion is not of God for He is not the author of confusion. You, too, were confused when you were in the world, but since you have come out from among those who are in the world, you have a more abundant life. You are free from the spirit of confusion if you stay connected and in communion with Jesus, the Christ.

– 8 –

The Voice in the Cup of the Flesh

" **F** or all that *is* in the world, the lust of the flesh, and the lust of the eyes, and the pride of life, is not of the Father, but is of the world" (1 John 2:16 KJV).

Flesh does not have the mind of God; nonetheless, it tries to speak as if it is the ambassador of God. It is a pretender, and it has its own distinct voice. It carries many labels—*selfish, self-centered, egotistical,* and even *narcissistic.* It is vain, boastful, and opinionated. It cares nothing about others' well-being. It has a grandiose sense of self-importance; it expects others to offer it special favors and fulfill its demands without question. Flesh believes that it is special. It seats itself in high places, constantly craving and demanding attention. It craves the adoration, praise, and worship due unto God. Flesh forgets that it stinks and is destined for the grave. There is nothing good about flesh.

Flesh boasts about everything. It seats itself too high to be reached, and it can only fall—and what a great fall it is. It is very deceived and deceiving. It is a liar and a traitor. It lusts for forbidden things without any remorse, and it indulges in unspeakable behaviors. It cares nothing for those it hurts. This is the reason Jesus said to crucify the flesh daily and follow Him. "And he said to them all, If any man will come after me, let him deny himself, and take up his cross daily, and follow" (Luke 9:23 KJV). You must deny your flesh. Tell the flesh to be silent. Just recently, my flesh was speaking something contrary to the Word of God, and I just told it, "Peace! Be still in the name of Jesus. I am not on speaking terms with you." You can talk to the flesh. Make it bend and bow down to the will of God in your life. If you don't, you will be betrayed by it constantly.

Flesh will woo you and romance you into a devilish lifestyle. It is incredibly charming, and it gives you a distorted view. If you are not careful, you will become enamored by it, and before you know it, you will have made it your idol and believe the lie it tells you that you do not need the Savior, Jesus Christ. What a liar it is! The flesh is vicious and unteachable, and with its idealized self-image, it does not take too kindly to any sort of instruction, nor does it appreciate disapproval. It does not admit faults when it is wrong, and it cannot handle criticism, whether it is constructive or otherwise.

Flesh has a language of its own. It is of the world, and it is worldly. You must learn to recognize it. It is loud, obnoxious, and ignorant. It makes itself an "enthroned king" in the person, body, soul, and spirit. It is prideful and admits to no error. It is perfect in its own eyes. Its distorted view of perfection is what causes it to lust after all the things that will earn the eternal spirit a one-way ticket to hell. It doesn't care, because it will not inherit the kingdom of heaven. It cannot handle the pure and holy. It is not created to withstand purity, nor is it created for holiness. It is corruptible. "In a moment, in the twinkling of an eye, at the last trump: for the trumpet shall sound, and the dead shall be raised incorruptible, and we shall be changed" (1 Cor. 15:53 KJV).

In the cup of flesh is nothing but corruption. Its work is rotten. Can you see it calling your attention? It screams, "Hear me!" Can you smell it? It stinks, doesn't it? It must be a stench to your nostrils as it is to God's. I say, crucify it! It is not your friend; it is your enemy. It does not have a servant's heart. It wants you to serve it. It desires immorality and all that is repugnant. It works with Satan and its demons against your spirit. Get a hold of it and make known to it that you are the boss. You can do this. Just command it to be silent, bow down, and serve you as you serve the living God. "Now the works of the flesh are manifest, which are these; Adultery, fornication, uncleanness, lasciviousness, idolatry, witchcraft, hatred, variance, emulations, wrath, strife, seditions, heresies, envyings, murders, drunkenness, revelings, and such like: of the which I tell you before, as I have also told you in time past, that they which do such things shall not inherit the kingdom of God" (Gal. 5:19–21 KJV).

I remember a sister in Christ named Lovita who suffered from the python spirit. She loved to gossip. She frequently attended a prayer group meeting of which I was a part, and she brought the "prayer" request each meeting. I was very concerned and sought the Lord on how to handle the situation. One day, I said to Lovita, "Sis, just tell your flesh to stop talking." To my amazement, she did without any hesitation. Afterward, I said to her, "Now, what was it you wanted to tell us?" She replied, "I don't remember." That put an end to the gossip.

Flesh works with the enemy to stop the work of the Lord. You must recognize it and silence it before it does damage. This is something that must be done daily. Remember, Jesus told us to crucify the flesh and follow Him. Flesh must die and stay dead if you are to follow Christ Jesus and work for the kingdom of your God and King. Thank God for making a way of escape. "There hath no temptation taken you but such as is common to man: but God is faithful, who will not suffer you to be tempted above that ye are able; but will with the temptation also make a way to escape, that ye may be able to bear it." (1 Cor. 10:13 KJV).

The voice in the cup of the flesh speaks corruption, but thank God you can trade everything it speaks with the voice of the cup of the Lord. Receive the blessings provided by Jesus the Christ instead of the despicable provision of the voice of flesh. Trade the contents of your cup of flesh for the gifts of God.

Husbands and wives, trade your adultery for loyalty, and let the love of God fill all your heart's desires. Only He can fill the emptiness of your heart. Men and women cannot fill the space belonging to God. They are but temporary fixes. Sooner or later, you will find yourself in someone else's arms lusting for more. Your needs cannot be met by flesh. Let God take His place on the throne of your heart. Then and only then will you be able to love and be loved. Fornication is not the way. It never was. It will leave you devastated, confused, and looking for the next victim. It is not satisfying. It is degrading and not God's will for your life. Ask God to put your sexual desires to sleep until the right one—the one He created just for you—comes. Come out from your uncleanness and be washed and purified by the blood of the Lamb of God.

Leave your pernicious ways of lasciviousness and fasten yourself to the love of the Father. He will not turn you away but will embrace you and love you right into His kingdom of heaven. Turn from idolatry and serve, praise, and worship God and Him alone. God does not share you with idols. He must be the One and the only One in your life. You know idols are deaf and dumb. They cannot help you. Every one of them will bow down to God even as Dagon did in the presence of the Ark of God in 1 Samuel 5:1–7 and 17. Keep your heart pure and your hands clean and away from witchcraft.

Witchcraft is evil and the work of the enemy. It will keep you and others in bondage. Magic, whether white or black, is of the flesh and of the devil. Keep your hands clean and away from this evil. God is not pleased with those who practice witchcraft, and those who do not repent, as already seen, will have the fate of hellfire. Pray against this evil in your life and in the lives of those in your bloodline. Pray against this spirit of witchcraft in your local church as well. Many who practice witchcraft have infiltrated the local churches, and they must be stopped from corrupting God's house. They have two choices—be set free or leave. Do it in God's love, but if they do not receive, do not tolerate them or they will destroy your church. Stay in God's love, and do not hate anyone. Help those you can along the way, and as for those you cannot help, pray for them. There is a lot of strife in the world, but you keep yourself clean and away from this evil. Variation is not of God, and it will cause you to stumble. Turn your back on variation and treat all as you want to be treated. Disparity grieves our God's and Father's heart. Therefore, stay constant in God's love for all. After all, you are commanded to love. Be angry and sin not. God holds you accountable for all you say and do. Keep peace with all people when possible. Know that God honors those who keep His love flowing to others. Do not adopt a spirit of rivalries and strife, and turn away from seditions to faithfulness and peace, unspeakable peace that surpasses all understanding.

You know that heresies and the doctrine of Christ Jesus do not mix or mingle. Therefore, keep your eyes on the prize, and stay in continual fellowship with Jesus, the Christ. Do not envy. God is good, and He is your provider. He has provided everything you need and will ever need. Stealing, killing, and destroying spirits are not of God.

Be happy and grateful for what you have. He supplies all your needs in Christ Jesus. He is a good Father. "But my God shall supply all your need according to his riches in glory by Christ Jesus" (Phil. 4:19 KJV). When you envy, you adopt a murdering spirit. Don't be deceived. Let love connect you to the Spirit of love in Father God and bring abundant life to you. Be filled with God's Holy Spirit instead of wine, and let your drunken spirit go for it is for the ungodly revelings, the uninformed, and the ignorant. It serves no purpose in the kingdom of God.

The cup of flesh, as we have seen, contains nothing but deadly impurities that guarantee you hell, but the wisdom of God delivers to you heaven, eternal life with your God and Father. Trade the cup of flesh for the cup of righteousness and the kingdom of heaven.

Heaven is the place you want to spend eternity. In heaven there are no tears, no death, no pain, no sorrow, and no suffering. It is a place of rest and of peace, a perfect and holy place. "And God shall wipe away all tears from their eyes, and there shall be no more death, neither sorrow, nor crying, neither shall there be any more pain; for the former things are passed away" (Rev. 21:4 KJV).

Eternal life with God started the day you accepted His Son Jesus Christ as your Lord and Savior. Jesus said that He went to prepare a place for you, and He will come back for you. "Let not your heart be troubled: ye believe in God, believe also in me. In my Father's house are many mansions: if it were not so, I would have told you. I go to prepare a place for you. And if I go and prepare a place for you, I will come again, and receive you unto myself; that where I am, there ye may be also. And whither I go ye know, and the way ye know" (John 14:1–4 KJV).

You are not an orphan. Your Father God wants you to come home someday and join Him. This is where you belong. Heaven is an amazing and beautiful place made of jewels and streets of gold. I remember visiting an idol temple many years ago with a floor made of silver. Impressive, right? No! Just as I started thinking of the fact that I was standing on a floor made of silver, the Lord reminded me of the streets of gold in heaven. Immediately, I was back to my senses and was not impressed with the devil's counterfeit (Rev. 21 KJV).

Once you believe and confess Jesus as your Lord and Savior, you can be certain of your eternity in heaven. Jesus, the sacrificial Lamb and High Priest, is the sacrifice offered and the High Priest who offered His blood sacrificed to the Father for you. "But this man, after he had offered one sacrifice for sins for ever, sat down on the right hand of God" (Heb. 10:12 KJV). Jesus gave His life and blood to purchase your eternal life with the Father, and your name is written in the Lamb's book of life. He will not blot it out. Jesus's blood washed you and made you clean. You have nothing to fear. Just believe! Nothing impure will ever enter heaven, nor will anyone who does what is shameful or deceitful, but only those whose names are written in the Lamb's book of life. "And there shall in no wise enter into it any thing that defileth, neither whatsoever worketh abomination, or maketh a lie: but they which are written in the Lamb's book of life" (Rev. 21:27 KJV).

Silence flesh and embrace the voice of the Spirit of the living God. Hold tightly to God's Spirit. He will guide you and lead you into all truth. Flesh can only lie to fulfill its lustful desires, but the Holy Spirit will counsel you and teach you all things pertaining to Father God and His kingdom, your heavenly abode. "But the Comforter, which is the Holy Ghost, whom the Father will send in my name, he shall teach you all things, and bring all things to your remembrance, whatsoever I have said unto you" (John 14:26 KJV).

– 9 –

The Voice in the Staggering Cup

L ife is full of choices, and you have been given quite a few in this study. Again, you are to make the decision on what cup to partake from: the staggering cup or the communion cup. Scriptures tell you not to be drunk with wine but to be filled with the Spirit of God. "And be not drunk with wine, wherein is excess; but be filled with the Spirit; Speaking to yourselves in psalms and hymns and spiritual songs, singing and making melody in your heart to the Lord. Giving thanks always for all things unto God and the Father in the name of our Lord Jesus Christ" (Eph. 5:18–20 KJV).

You can be merry in the Holy Spirit. Have you ever experienced the Spirit of laughter? I have. It is the most fun experience ever. You can get totally drunk in the Spirit, and the best part of it is that you do not wake up with a hangover. The heart is glad and filled with joy, unspeakable joy. That is what drinking from the Holy Spirit does for you. This experience makes you bolder and stronger in the Lord. Why look to the spirits? Aren't that what alcoholic beverages are called? Have you ever wondered why they are called spirits? Could it be that, perhaps, they alter people's behavior and cause them to display unwanted character traits because they are under the influence, as some refer to the experience? Whose influence is it? Could it be that it is the influence of demons? And that is the reason many overindulge uncontrollably, lose their sense of right and wrong, and do vile things. This is the staggering cup in which many indulge and later pay dearly, for the consequences are detrimental. God warns of these things, and you must listen and take heed. "Rejoice and be glad, O daughter of Edom, that dwellest in the land of Uz; the cup also shall pass through unto thee: thou shalt be drunken, and shalt make thyself naked. The punishment of thine iniquity is accomplished, O daughter of Zion; he will no more carry thee away into captivity: he will visit thine iniquity, O daughter of Edom; he will discover thy sins" (Lam. 4:21–22 KJV).

Overindulging is dangerous. Whether or not you find yourself in captivity is a matter of time. Many have become addicted to alcohol and have lost everything because of it. Would you agree with me that they are in bondage? Of course they are. Some have drunk themselves to death, while others are in prison because their judgment lapsed, they drove drunk, and they killed someone or many people. Yet others are homeless and have lost their families because the addiction has a tight grip on them and they have not been able to escape. Let us continuously pray for their deliverance.

Although the enemy makes it look good, the staggering cup has nothing good in it. All it contains are headaches and hardships. Therefore, you must not partake of it. It will only destroy you. Self-inflicted pain is as deadly as that inflicted by others, and the end results are similar if not the same. Do unto others as you would have them do unto you. God is omnipresent, and He sees all things. Don't be surprised when you find yourself in a pickle because you did not heed the warning signs and the conviction of the Holy Spirit. "Thou hast shewed thy people hard things: thou hast made us to drink the wine of astonishment" (Ps. 60:3 KJV). Don't be prideful. Cry out to God, and He will deliver you. He hears prayers and He is merciful. Run from the staggering cup and to His communion cup.

– 10 –

The Voice in the Cup
of Communion

We have talked about not partaking of the cup of demons and instead partaking of the cup of the Lord. "Ye cannot drink the cup of the Lord, and the cup of devils: ye cannot be partakers of the Lord's table, and the table of devils" (1 Cor. 10:21 KJV). In the cup of the Lord rest our Blessings, which can be received through communion with the Lord. At the Lord's Supper, also called the Lord's Table, you find nourishment for your body, for your soul and your spirit: "The cup of blessing which we bless, is it not the communion of the blood of Christ? The bread which we break, is it not the communion of the body of Christ?" (1 Cor. 10:16 NKJV). "And they continued steadfastly in the apostles' doctrine and fellowship, and in breaking of bread, and in prayers" (Acts 2:42 NKJV). In the early Church it was also called *Eucharist*, or "giving of thanks. "And he took the cup, and gave thanks, and gave *it* to them, saying, Drink ye all of it" (Matt. 26:27 NKJV).

The account of when Jesus instituted this ordinance of communion is given in scriptures, as you have already seen. However, to have a better understanding of communion, let's look at its contents and the purpose behind the act. The elements used to represent both Christ's body and Christ's blood are bread and wine, respectively. The kind of bread is not specified. Christ used unleavened bread symbolic of His body. Wine is used to represent the shed blood of Christ. Jesus did this at the Last Supper. He wanted His disciples to receive communion as a remembrance of Him to commemorate His death.

Communion signifies, seals, and applies to believers all the benefits of the new covenant. In the ordinance, Jesus ratifies His promises to His people, and for their part, they solemnly consecrate themselves to Him and to the work of the kingdom. It is a badge of Christian profession. In addition, communion indicates and promotes the communion of believers with Christ Jesus, and it represents the mutual communion of believers with one another. Having said that, how do you prepare for communion? You must be born again, having received Jesus Christ as your Lord and Savior and as a disciple following the doctrine or teaching of Jesus Christ. "And when he had given thanks, he brake [it], and said, Take, eat: this is my body, which is broken for you: this do in remembrance of me. After the same manner also [he took] the cup, when he had supped, saying, This cup is the new testament in my blood: this do ye, as oft as ye drink [it], in remembrance of me. For as often as ye eat this bread, and drink this cup, ye do shew the Lord's death till he come" (1 Cor. 11:24–26 KJV). Here, Jesus is talking to His disciples and not to the world.

The Bible warns you about receiving the communion unworthily. For he who eats and drinks in an unworthy manner eats and drinks judgment to himself, not discerning the Lord's body. "For this reason many *are* weak and sick among you, and many sleep. For if we would judge ourselves, we would not be judged. But when we are judged, we are chastened by the Lord, that we may not be condemned with the world" (1 Cor. 11:29–32 NKJV). Because of these scriptures, a lot of churches' observations of communion is preceded by a time of introspection, usually with a serious cautionary statement given by the pastor and a time of confession, in which people will stand up or come forward to confess sins they have committed or to ask forgiveness from others in the congregation. Although it is a good idea for Christians to identify sin in their lives and repent of it, the Bible does not make this a requirement for participation in communion.

I remember attending a church where, every time communion was served, we had to go to one another and make things right. For the most part, I had nothing against anyone. I kept and keep a clear heart by the conviction of the Holy Spirit. However, when people came to me to make things right for themselves, it made me feel dirty and in need of a bath in the blood of Jesus for cleansing. They were at times very detailed and about some very petty stuff that just did not need to be addressed—at least, not with me. This church had a viper spirit running rampant. And it was a lot of "he said, she said." I did not enjoy the communion time with this group. It kept things stirred up.

Of course, I have had to ask the Lord to forgive me, but that religious act was disturbing. The same people did not change, and they continued to perform the act expected by the pastor every time. Somehow, the purpose of communion was lost in the act. Yes, you must examine your own heart and make sure it is clean and ready for communion. It is something that must be done daily and not just at communion time. And when you know that it is communion Sunday, don't wait for the last minute to get things right with God and people. We took communion on the first Sunday of the month, so why not live a clean life or take care of business immediately? Why wait for the first Sunday of the month?

Even though the practice was disturbing to me, I had to keep reminding myself that I was not fighting with flesh and blood but with evil spirits. I had to continue loving the people and praying for them and for me, but I hated the spirits behind their behavior. I prayed constantly for unity and for increased discernment of spirits in all of us so we could see the forces behind our discord, put them to flight, and live in peace and in harmony with one another.

– 11 –

The Fire of Hell

"**U**pon the wicked He will rain snares, fire and brimstone, and an horrible tempest; this shall be the portion of their cup" (Ps. 11:6 KJV).

We spoke briefly about hell, but it needs a little bit more attention. I have heard people joke about hell and how much fun they are going to have there. Some think they will be drinking, having illicit sex, and just having a "good old' time." Wake up and smell hell. It is not that kind of place. Satan and his demons have deceived you into this type of erroneous thinking. The Word of God is clear in its description of hell. After you have read this book, you will have no more excuses and no more surprises. Hell is hell. It is not the fun place you have been tricked into believing.

"But on the day that Lot went out of Sodom it rained fire and brimstone from heaven and destroyed *them* all" (Luke 17:29 KJV).

Although you cannot ask the residents of Sodom and Gomorrah and the surrounding cities what happened, you can read the account for yourself. They too thought it was all fun and games until judgment came. Many today have sided with the government and have neglected the truth of the Word of God, but that is temporary. Eternity is just that— eternity. It has no end. Do you want to have the so-called fun for a few years and then burn in hell's fire for eternity? No, I think not. You are smarter than that. Don't believe the lies.

Look at what Jesus says in the following scripture: "If your hand or foot causes you to sin, cut it off and cast it from you. It is better for you to enter into life lame or maimed, rather than having two hands or two feet, to be cast into the everlasting fire" (Matt. 18:8 KJV).

Jesus makes it plain and simple. None will have any excuse at all before the Father on the day of judgment. He has paid the price, and all you must do is believe and receive His gift of eternal life. "Then He will also say to those on the left hand, 'Depart from Me, you cursed, into the everlasting fire prepared for the devil and his angels" (Matt. 25:41 NKJV). Again, hell was not made for God's people created in His image. It was and is for Satan and his demons. Keep your heart pure, your hands clean, and your eyes on Jesus, doing all that He commanded through the anointing of His Holy Spirit.

Live in peace with all people, forgiving one another and helping one another, for this is the way people will know that you are Christ's. Even though you do not work for your salvation, you still need to conduct yourself in a godly manner. Keep forgiving people and helping them as often as you can in Jesus. That is what Jesus did. The body of Christ must be connected to the head, Jesus Christ. Without Him you are but a dead body. He is the life in you. As He lives in you, you exhibit His character and do as Jesus did by living in God's love. When you abide in Jesus and Jesus in you, you do not have to fear anything. Love is stronger than any hate you may encounter or must face. God is love, and He has no equal.

"But I say to you that whoever is angry with his brother without a cause shall be in danger of the judgment. And whoever says to his brother, 'Raca!' shall be in danger of the council. But whoever says, 'You fool!' shall be in danger of hell fire" (Matt. 5:22 NKJV).

The story of the rich man and Lazarus clearly states that no one is coming back from the dead, despite some religions' claim that reincarnation is the way. You must do all the good you can while you are here on Earth. I always say that if you cannot do good to help people, leave them alone but pray for them with sincerity of heart. You never know what the future holds. "Then he cried and said, 'Father Abraham, have mercy on me, and send Lazarus that he may dip the tip of his finger in water and cool my tongue; for I am tormented in this flame" (Luke 16:24 NKJV).

This rich man closed his eyes to Lazarus's needs daily. Now in torment, he needed Lazarus, yet, still where he was, not much had changed because he still saw Lazarus as subservient to him. To his astonishment, Lazarus was not permitted to cross over to his side of torment. Don't be like the rich man; be kind to people. That is your reasonable duty. Use your God-given gifts and talents to make a difference in the world. Lend a helping hand. It will pay off in the end. God's rewards and punishments are true, and they are real. "And they shall go forth and look upon the corpses of the men who have transgressed against Me. For their worm does not die. And their fire is not quenched. They shall be an abhorrence to all flesh" (Isa. 66:24 NKJV).

"He himself shall also drink of the wine of the wrath of God, which is poured out full strength into the cup of His indignation. He shall be tormented with fire and brimstone in the presence of the holy angels and in the presence of the Lamb" (Rev. 14:10 NKJV).

"Then the beast was captured, and with him the false prophet who worked signs in his presence, by which he deceived those who received the mark of the beast and those who worshiped his image. These two were cast alive into the lake of fire burning with brimstone" (Rev. 19:20 NKJV).

"The devil, who deceived them, was cast into the lake of fire and brimstone where the beast and the false prophet *are*. And they will be tormented day and night forever and ever" (Rev. 20:10 NKJV).

"Then Death and Hades were cast into the lake of fire. This is the second death" (Rev. 20:14 NKJV).

Here you find a list of those who behave in such manners as those who will not inherit the kingdom of heaven and will suffer the punishment of hell. The key to escaping the fire of hell is obedience to God's Word. Follow Christ's doctrine, and it will go well with you. As you look at the things here, pause and examine your heart; only you and the Holy Spirit can do this. Should you find yourself in any of these categories, it is not too late. Take a minute and ask the Holy Spirit to help you. He will. Ask God for forgiveness, receive His forgiveness, and turn away from your wicked ways. Remember, He will throw that sin or sins into the depths of the sea, and He will not remember any of it ever again. "He will turn again, he will have compassion upon us; he will subdue our iniquities; and thou will cast all their sins into the depths of the sea" (Micah 7:19 KJV). Now, if He doesn't remember it, neither should you. Walk in the freedom and liberty purchased and provided for you by the blood of Jesus Christ His Son, your Savior and deliverer.

"But the cowardly, unbelieving, abominable, murderers, sexually immoral, sorcerers, idolaters, and all liars shall have their part in the lake which burns with fire and brimstone, which is the second death" (Rev. 21:8 NKJV). This is reserved for those who will not heed the Word of God and repent. It is not for Christians, believers in the teaching of Jesus Christ the Lord. This is not part of the cup of the Lord. It is part of the fierce cup of anger and wrath of God prepared for Satan, his demons, and those who disobey the Word of God. Your portion is that of His cup of salvation. *Drink up!*

– 12 –

God-Ordained Prayers: Salvation

T he Lord of salvation is knocking on your door. Open up, and welcome Him in.

> That if thou shalt confess with thy mouth the
> Lord Jesus, and shalt believe in thine heart
> that God hath raised him from the dead,
> thou shalt be saved. For with the heart man
> believeth unto righteousness; and with the
> mouth confession is made unto salvation. For
> the scripture saith, Whosoever believeth on
> him shall not be ashamed. For there is no
> difference between the Jew and the Greek: for
> the same Lord over all is rich unto all that

call upon him. For whosoever shall call upon
the name of the Lord shall be saved. (Rom.
10:9–13 KJV)

According to the Bible, we all have sinned and come short
of the glory of God (see Rom. 3:23). We all need the Savior,
Jesus Christ. We see in scriptures that all we need is to believe
with our hearts and confess with our mouths that God sent
Jesus Christ; that He was born of Virgin Mary; that He
was crucified, He died, and He was buried; and that He
went to hell and took the keys to Hades and death. "I *am* He
who lives, and was dead, and behold, I am alive forevermore.
Amen. And I have the keys of Hades and of Death" (Rev. 1:18
NKJV). Then, He was raised from the dead, or resurrected,
on the third day and ascended to heaven, and now He is
seated at the right hand of God interceding for us. If we
believe and confess all this, we will be saved. You are saved
when you believe in your heart and confess with your mouth.
Just do it. Salvation is yours for the believing and receiving.

Salvation Prayer

Lord Jesus,
I believe in my heart and I confess with my mouth that you
came and died for my sins. I ask you to forgive me of all my
sins and to come into my life and to become my Lord and
Savior. Thank you, Jesus, for forgiving me of all my sins and
for setting me free.

Now that you have prayed this prayer, if you do not already
have a Bible, invest in one. I recommend you purchase the

King James Version and that you begin to read the book of John followed by Romans. These are two good Bible books for new Christians. I also recommend you join a good Bible study group and a local church.

Water Baptism and Holy Spirit Baptism

After salvation, there are two other acts of obedience that you must follow. They are water baptism and Holy Spirit baptism. Even though one does not have to happen before the other, both must take place. They are both commanded by God. Let me clear something up before moving on: Jesus was both water baptized and Holy Spirit baptized. If Jesus did both baptisms, do you not think that you need them as well? Jesus is our greatest example. Those who say they don't need to be baptized make God to be a liar. He is the Spirit of truth and cannot ever lie because whatever He says happens. That means that you must do the right thing if you want to be in right standing with God the Father, God the Son, and God the Holy Spirit.

Jesus was water baptized by John the Baptist and filled with the Holy Spirit as He was coming out of the water, as seen in the scriptures, when the Spirit of God descended upon Him from above like a dove. The dove here is symbolic of the Holy Spirit. Immediately, the scriptures talk about God the Father validating Jesus as His beloved Son.

> Then cometh Jesus from Galilee to Jordan unto
> John, to be baptized of him. But John forbad
> him, saying, I have need to be baptized of thee,

and comest thou to me? And Jesus answering
said unto him, Suffer it to be so now: for thus
it becometh us to fulfil all righteousness.
Then he suffered him. And Jesus, when he
was baptized, went up straightway out of the
water: and, lo, the heavens were opened unto
him, and he saw the Spirit of God descending
like a dove, and lighting upon him: And lo a
voice from heaven, saying, This is my beloved
Son, in whom I am well pleased. (Matt. 3:13–
17 KJV)

Water and Holy Spirit baptisms are commended to us by
Jesus. Scriptures are clear on both. There really is no need
for interpretation on either one. Either you are obedient or
you are disobedient to the Word of God and Jesus, who is the
Word of God. "In the beginning was the Word, and the Word
was with God, and the Word was God" (John 1:1 KJV). We
cannot sugarcoat it, and we cannot whitewash it. It is what
it is. "Go ye therefore, and teach all nations, baptizing them
in the name of the Father, and of the Son, and of the Holy
Ghost: Teaching them to observe all things whatsoever I have
commanded you: and, lo, I am with you always, even unto the
end of the world. Amen" (Matt. 28:19–20 KJV).

Jesus commands us to go into all the world and to baptize people
in the name of the Father, the Son, and the Holy Spirit. You
cannot baptize anyone in the Holy Spirit if you have not been
baptized yourself. Normally, there aren't any problems with
water baptism. Most Christian churches believe in some type

of water baptism even if it is a sprinkling of water, which is not scripturally sound because Jesus, as our greatest example, had full-immersion water baptism. In this act of obedience, you are declaring to the world that you belong to Jesus. It denotes the washing of one's sins into the water, and as one comes out, that person is a Christian. Does the water have the power to cleanse us from sins? No! But, Jesus does, and He cleanses us from all unrighteousness and causes us to become in right standing with Him. Many have been healed during water baptism. God sees the obedient heart and heals His people because He loves those who honor Him. There are always blessings in obedience to our Lord Jesus Christ. Therefore, do not grieve the Holy Spirit.

When it comes to the baptism of the Holy Spirit, some are confused because of erroneous teachings, their own lack of knowledge, or the influence of Satan to keep God's people ignorant. The Bible says that God's people perish for lack of knowledge because they have rejected teaching. Christians must keep a teachable spirit if they want to please their Lord and Savior, Jesus Christ. "My people are destroyed for lack of knowledge: because thou hast rejected knowledge, I will also reject thee, that thou shalt be no priest to me: seeing thou hast forgotten the law of thy God, I will also forget thy children" (Hosea 4:6 KJV). The acceptance of the baptism of the Holy Spirit is one area people have forgotten. Again, Jesus told His disciples to tarry until they received power from above. These were people who sat under Jesus's direct teaching. How much more do we need the Holy Spirit today? "But ye shall receive power, after that the Holy Ghost is come upon you: and ye shall be witnesses unto me both in Jerusalem, and in all Judaea, and in Samaria, and unto the uttermost part of the earth" (Acts 1:8 KJV).

The Holy Spirit is the third Person of the Godhead. He is the comforter, the teacher, the counselor, and so much more. He is a person and a gentleman. He will never force Himself on anyone. You must make the choice to receive Him. He is a gift to you from Jesus even as Jesus is a gift to you from Father God.

Many say that people must be *clean* or *right* before receiving the Holy Spirit, but that is not true. I once witnessed a sorcerer receive the Holy Spirit. She had just accepted Jesus as her Lord and Savior but had not been delivered. I knew that she was a witch by the anointing of the Holy Spirit, so I asked the Lord to fill her with His Holy Spirit so her salvation could really take. It was then that the demons in her began acting out. It took seven men to hold her down. She was delivered, praise the Lord, and afterward, she was filled with the Holy Spirit. You see, the Holy Spirit had the right to her life because she had accepted Jesus, but He was not going to share a home with demons. He is holy, so He kicked them out and took His rightful place in her life. So you see, you do not have to be perfect to receive the Holy Spirit. That notion is a trick of the enemy, and believe me, he has many up his sleeves. I am not saying you have a demon; what I am saying is that you do not have to be perfect. The Holy Spirit is the One who cleanses you, not you yourself.

As you can see, the Holy Spirit is the One who helps you get your life together. Don't believe the lie. All have sinned and come short of the glory of God. You cannot live a righteous life without the Holy Spirit. You desperately need Him in your life. All you must do is believe what Jesus said and ask Jesus to baptize you with His Holy Spirit. This is an act of faith. Don't worry if you do not understand the utterance that comes with the baptism. God will not give you anything bad. "Or what man is there of you, whom if his son ask bread, will he give him a stone? Or if he ask a fish, will he give him a serpent? If ye then, being evil, know how to give good gifts unto your children, how much more shall your Father which is in heaven give good things to them that ask him?" (Matt. 7:9–11 KJV). He loves you, and speaking in tongues is the first evidence of being baptized with the Holy Spirit. You do not have to understand what you are saying—just trust Him.

You should receive the Holy Spirit the first time you ask Jesus, but if doesn't happen, don't give up. He will baptize you because it is of Him. "If a son shall ask bread of any of you that is a father, will he give him a stone? or if he ask a fish, will he for a fish give him a serpent? Or if he shall ask an egg, will he offer him a scorpion? If ye then, being evil, know how to give good gifts unto your children: how much more shall your heavenly Father give the Holy Spirit to them that ask him?" (Luke 11:11–13 KJV).

The Holy Spirit is a promise not only to a few select ones. He is the promise of Jesus for all who believe then, now, and until Jesus comes back for us. Do you believe? Then He is for you.

"For the promise is unto you, and to your children, and to all that are afar off, even as many as the LORD our God shall call" (Acts 2:39 KJV).

Water Baptism

Your pastor or minister will perform a water baptism in a baptistery, a pool, a river, or even in the ocean. The arrangement for your baptism are normally made ahead of time so that you can prepare for it. For this occasion, I recommend that men wear swim trunks and women wear a one-piece swimsuit under the garment. It will keep you and those around you from being embarrassed since wet clothes tend to become see-through. Usually, the minister will say something like, "I baptize you in the name of the Father, the Son, and the Holy Spirit" as you are being immersed in water. It is done very quickly, so don't be afraid of the water; just enjoy this experience with your Lord Jesus Christ. Don't be surprised if you have a special encounter during your water baptism, and don't be disappointed if nothing extraordinary happens. God knows what you need and when you need it.

Holy Spirit Baptism

Lord Jesus,
I believe you and your Word. I repent of all my sins, and I ask you to forgive me.
Lord, I know that according to your Word, Jesus, you have forgiven me, and you remember my sins no more. Thank you for forgiving me.
Lord, I forgive myself as well.

Lord Jesus, now I ask you to baptize me with your precious Holy Spirit.

Holy Spirit, I welcome you into my life. I honor you with my life, and I ask you to become my teacher, my counselor, my comforter, my protector, my everything.
Holy Spirit, thank you for coming into my life and being my teacher, my counselor, my comforter, my protector, my everything.

Now, open your mouth in faith, and let the Holy Spirit fill your mouth. You will feel a tingling in your tongue or mouth, and your jaws may feel a bit heavy. Don't worry; it is the Holy Spirit. He will speak through you if you just believe and humble yourself before Him.

Plead the Blood of Jesus

Plead is a legal term used in courts of law. You have heard of people pleading guilty or not guilty in the court of law; pleading the blood of Jesus works in a similar way. By pleading the blood of Jesus, you are saying that the blood paid for whatever it is that Satan is accusing you of, and because Jesus paid for your sins with His Blood, you are innocent. Satan is very legalistic, and he finds things in our lives that we didn't even know were there. Some things have been passed down to us by our ancestors or are foreign to us, but Satan knows about them and tries to use them against us. We can command Satan to flee from us by using the name of Jesus and the blood of Jesus. Jesus's blood is for our protection.

When Christians use the expression "plead the blood of Jesus," it simply means that they call on the blood of Jesus in prayer. By doing so, they are exercising their faith in all the benefits purchased by the blood of Jesus at Calvary for those who believe in the sacrifice of Christ's death. It is the blood of Jesus that Satan is afraid of, and he leaves them in peace because he knows what the blood represents. I recommend that you study the blood of Jesus in detail and believe in it. When you do and you apply the blood of Jesus, Satan has no other choice but to flee from your presence and from your life. It is in the power of the blood that salvation, healing, deliverance, and all provisions are made for you and for me. I am alive today because of the blood of Jesus. I have had demons try to harass me, and each time, all I had to say is, "The blood of Jesus is against you, Satan," and the demons he had sent after me left immediately. The blood works. Believe in its power. It is the power of God, and it is the difference in Christians' lives. You have the name and the blood of Jesus along with the Holy Spirit on your side. Be of good courage.

Communion Prayer

Say this prayer out loud, for there is power in the spoken word. Pick up the bread and communion cup and say this prayer with me.

Father God, thank you for sending your Son, Jesus Christ, to die for me and make a way for me to live for you and with you forever.

Thank you, Lord Jesus, for giving your life to save mine. I am forever grateful to you.

Holy Spirit, thank you for coming and sealing me with salvation.

Father, in the name of your Son Jesus Christ, I repent of my sins and ask you to forgive me for against you have I sinned.

Father, thank you for forgiving me of all my sins and for not remembering them ever again.

Lord, I choose to receive my forgiveness, and I forgive myself as well.

Lord, I pick up the bread, break it, and eat it in your precious Name, Jesus.

Lord Jesus, I lift up the cup, and I drink it in your powerful name, Jesus.

I do this out of obedience to the Word of God and in remembrance of you, my Lord Jesus Christ, until you return.

Lord, thank you for your incorruptible and powerful blood.

Amen!

CONCLUSION

In conclusion, there are many speaking voices attempting to communicate with us at any given time. Sometimes they try to speak to us violently. Other times, they try to speak to us softly. No matter how they attempt to communicate with us, we must use discernment in identifying the speaking voice or voices. To that end, we have looked at the voices in each cup. I pray you heard the voices but chose to communicate and to commune with the voice in the cup of the Lord, the cup of blessings, reconciling you back to the Father into a better relationship and a more intimate fellowship and times of praise and worship with Him. The cup is yours to partake from daily. Jesus shed His blood to purchase you back to the Father from a life of sins. He brought you from the kingdom of darkness into His marvelous kingdom of light.

Now that you are on His side, you receive bread and wine in communion in the church of Jesus Christ and in your home in remembrance of Him until He comes again. Jesus is coming back soon, and you need to be ready. You do not know the hour, but you do know that He is soon to come. The descriptions of hell, hellfire, and the fierce anger cup of the wrath of God were not intended to horrify you but to give you a picture of a place you never want to be in. And according to the Word of God, Jesus provided a way for you to escape hell and all it contains. Thank Jesus for His cup of suffering and your cup of salvation and blessings. I pray this study has been a blessing to you as it was for me. Stay hungry for the Word of God, stay thirsty for the Lord Jesus, and drink from the cup of the Lord often.

A Prayer for the Believers

Heavenly Father,

I come to you in your Son Jesus's name and covered in His precious blood. I thank you for the fulfillment of your Word concerning this book. I pray, Father, that you open the spiritual eyes of all who read this book to see the miracles in your teachings. I pray they apply your every word to their lives and fulfill your purpose in their lives. I pray they know in their minds that your gifts and calling are without repentance. Father, open the windows of heaven and pour out blessings upon them so they may have the relationship you desire with them for they are your children. Bless them with a thirst and hunger for your Word and for you. I release your blessings upon their lives. I agree with you, Father, that they are blessed, and I pray they know it. Cause them to be instruments of glory in your hands. Open their eyes to see that there are no limitations with you and they can go far above and beyond all they have imagined as they allow your Holy Spirit to lead them in all truth. Let them see themselves in Jesus, even as Jesus is in you. Let them become one with you and in you to fulfill your kingdom work. Let them walk in tune with your heart's desire, moving with your every heartbeat. All this I pray, and I know my prayers are answered because you are the author of this prayer and you always hear me. I seal this book and this prayer in Jesus's name and by the anointing of the Holy Spirit with the fire of God and the blood of Jesus. Amen!

Printed in the United States
By Bookmasters